WALKING WITH

STEVEN ZIMMERMAN
WITH MELISA ZIMMERMAN

We want to hear from you. Please send any comments you have about this book to info@bridgebuildermm.org

Walking With ~~Dog~~ God
Copyright 2013 by Bridge Builder Marriage Ministry
Requests for information should be addressed to:

Bridge Builder Marriage Ministry
www.bridgebuildermm.org

All Scriptures quotations, unless otherwise indicated, are taken from the Holy Bible, New International Version or Amplified Versions.
Photos taken by: Trent Dugas Photography and Katie Johnstonbaugh
Cover Design by Ashlee Roedell
Book Design by Paul Speir

Published by Speir Publishing
ISBN 13: 978-0-9826765-3-0
ISBN 10: 0982676530

All rights reserved. No part of the publication may be reproduced, stored in a retrieval system, or transmitted in any form or by any means without the prior written consent of Bridge Builder Marriage Ministry.

This book is dedicated to:
Alma Groninger, my eyes and ears;
Eileen Zimmerman, my inspiration and encouragement;
Melisa, my heart and soul.

Forward

Believe me when I tell you I had no idea about this adventure until I was right in the middle of it. Here is how it happened.

There are dog people, there are cat people, and there are people-people. My wife has had pets most of her life. My pet owning as a child was short lived and regulated by a contract that my father, the international contract lawyer, drew up telling us what we had to do and how we had to do it if we were going to keep a dog in our house. My brother, my two sisters, and I failed miserably living up to its terms. Our dog was seemingly whisked away in the middle of the night by the bad pet owner, Gestapo, never to be seen again.

This began many years without a bark, woof, or even a meow in my life. Things went along swimmingly without a hitch. There was no sense of loss for the absence of canines in my life.

Walking With God

There was, however, a gnawing in my gut. I lived a pretty good life, but something was missing. My best guess, which is the best guess of most guys, was I needed a woman. It sadly, wasn't the best answer. The correct answer was I needed a relationship with God. I knew God like I knew my history teacher. I liked him well enough and knew what room I could find him in, but I certainly couldn't claim to have a relationship with him. Unbeknownst to me, in typical, "His ways are higher than my ways" fashion, the secret to finding her, my soul-mate, with whom fifty years together seems like I'm cheating myself out of something would be a relationship with Him. She wouldn't touch me with a ten-foot pole if I didn't know in a real way, the Father, the Son, and the Holy Spirit. I opened the door to God; He opened the door to Melisa. Melisa opened the door to Raggs, Cooper, Cash, Gertie, Dutchess, Elizabeth Taylor, Riley, Duke, and Bernice.

Some dogs are better on leashes than others and we have several small breed dogs we didn't walk. This is the story of those we did. More importantly, it's how God started showing up on our walks and like Balaam's donkey (Numbers 22), He used the true companions to speak to us and share His wisdom. He gave us so much insight everyday that I eventually started journaling it so we wouldn't forget. Journaling also gave us a chance to share it with

Steven Zimmerman

others. It was a blog before blogging was cool. Here is a collection of the knowledge God dropped on us during the early hours as we walked our dogs and He walked with us. I hope you enjoy reading it as much as I enjoyed writing it.

February 3rd
Walking With Dog

We aren't really at day one; this is just the first time we are recording our conversations with God. Melisa and I got our Airedales at the end of December. We've walked them faithfully every morning, save the occasional ice storm. Little did we know it was going to be more about building our faith than toning our muscles.

We started our walks as a time to be together and talk without interruption. Our plans are not God's plan, however, the interruption came and it couldn't be ignored. God started showing up every morning and my wife, being the wise woman she is, (Proverbs 18:22) made a point of welcoming Him. So it became the five of us for 1.6 miles then eventually turning into 2.2 miles through our little town of 800 people in the middle of nowhere Oklahoma. Melisa and Elizabeth Taylor, Steve and Dutchess, and God going on our merry way.

Walking With God

Today is my birthday and I was blessed with sleeping in until 8am. I woke up with a word from God that he had something great for us on our walk today. I was so excited for it, that I forsook my morning coffee and got right into my walking clothes. It was lucky my walking clothes hadn't walked off by themselves. I'd been wearing the same ones; two pair of sweatpants, long-sleeved T-shirt and sweatshirt with cuffs all week long. Melisa was on the phone with her best friend Mary, whom she had not spoken to in a week. They were full throttle in conversation. She realized right away where I was at, without skipping a beat she dressed in her walking clothes, talking all the while always the multi-tasker, my wife. Before I blinked she was ready to go.

I made the decision to include my 17-year-old son, Levon's dog, Cash with us. I'm a novice dog owner and since we'd had a lot of ice lately, Cash had been neglected. We started our walks by taking our four dogs; Melisa had Elizabeth Taylor, 50 pounds of Airedale and Gertrude D. Rockefeller, 10 pounds of Shih-Tzu who belonged to our 10-year old daughter, Mariah. I had Dutchess, an Airedale weighing in at 50 pounds and Cash, a golden retriever/yellow lab mix at a fit and trim 85 pounds. Handling that much dog on the ice had left Cash inside for the better part of a couple of weeks. A new dog owner walking 135 pounds of dog on a fresh sheet of ice just wasn't happening.

So out we went this morning; bright sun, dry pavement (for the most part), and very little wind, a rarity here in Oklahoma (thank the Lord) and we headed out with great expectations. We were walking and I got in my mind about being nice to people, not a dizzying concept. I thought about going to the local quick shop is called Crossroads to buy ice and be friendly to the cashier. No special training required, no PhD., or extraordinary talent needed. We can all be nice. I called it sowing joy. What you sow you reap. An eternal principle; always true.

We have struggled, me especially living in Lookeba. Out in the sticks where we live, farmers surround us. God brought my attention to this; all around us people are sowing cotton, peppers, peanuts, wheat, and other crops. God just said, "Hey slowpoke, here's a giant visual aid. You need to sow. All The Time!" If I don't have money, clothing or something material to sow I can sow love, joy, peace and the fruit of the Spirit (Galatians 5:22-23). About this time, Cash, who is the pack-leader in the dog community at our house, tried to assert some dominance over me by pulling at his leash. I was about to put the beat-down on this usually gentle giant when the Spirit told me to sow patience – The Living Word of God in my life now applying a Bible truth with a practical use. I sowed the patience

Walking With God

and in the pinball machine that is my brain, the ideas started ricocheting.

Sowing good seed like patience will allow my soul to prosper. 3 John 2 says, "I will prosper and be in health even as my soul prospers." I am a bill collector and if I sow patience, I reap patience. You really need patience when trying to get someone to pay an eight-year old income tax bill they didn't even know they owed because the notice from the state was sent to an old address. I reap patience sown with Cash and the harvest allows me to reap at work because I have the spiritual tools needed to deal with people. My cost, kindness with Cash; my reward is a larger bonus check, cash. No rocket science just God's principle applied in my life. But wait it gets better!

The other types of "crops" out here in Western Oklahoma are oil, crude, black gold, and Texas tea. Melisa recently made the acquaintance of Bud Cox, a local pastor of a small, but extremely active church in neighboring Hinton. The church has about 35 people, but they have a food pantry, a prison ministry, and homeless program. They invest, read sow, into people's lives. God showed us that we needed to do something for Bud. We love our huge church in the big city, but Melisa is bonkers about how in love with God and his love of serving, Bud Cox is. We decided we needed to tap into his pipeline. Bud will enrich our lives. Our harvest from sowing into him will be many-fold. Bud is black, a rarity out here. He is our oil well. He is black gold out in the oil rich Western Oklahoma farmland. The spiritual wealth we draw from that relationship, coupled with our church, and our own relationship with an awesome God who spent our entire walk with us will lift us to a higher level, so what did we do?

We got home and called Bud to ask him out to lunch. We'll go through our closet today to donate clothing to his homeless ministry. I mentioned earlier that it is my birthday today, not without reason. I'm getting no material presents for my birthday. I am getting two date nights with my wife. I have plenty of clothes, music, movies, and books as it is. I will get the gift of sowing, and the benefits of reaping down the road. Investing time and love in my wife has yielded an incredible harvest, a marriage that has never waned. Happy Birthday to me!

February 4th
That's Fabulous!
Who's Your Designer?

Another 2.2 miles in the book and since we got the dogs Melisa and I have each walked the requisite 26.2 miles for a marathon in 30 minutes blocks. You might think a 13-hour time isn't very good, but it's better than the race that is never run.

We got up ready to walk and as we crested the little slope at the end of our driveway there sitting atop the horizon was a glorious sun. Greeting us, letting us know we would not freeze our tushes off like we did yesterday. As a transplanted Minnesotan, I should laugh at the Oklahoma winter, but I have to admit I've grown soft. These walks are a great way for me to reclaim my winter toughness.

I've always seen the sun as a representation of Jesus, the Son, so when it was the first thing I noticed before

Steven Zimmerman

I turned down Sickles Avenue I knew there'd be no shortage of material to write about this morning. A faithful God delivered as promised. I very nearly called today "God loves Lynyrd Skynyrd." Here's why; we started our walk talking about a conversation Melisa had with her brother Mike and his wife Lindsey about a book entitled, "Driven by Eternity" by John Bevere that we are leading a small group about. It was profoundly challenging her beliefs about heaven and how you get there and what happens once you are there. Mike and Lindsey both come from highly religious backgrounds and are gun-shy about being preached to. It is our prayer that everyone, including Mike and Lindsey, come in the to kind of relationship with God where taking walks with Him or driving to work with Him is as comfortable as your favorite pair of jeans or my old black leather jacket Melisa wants me to throw away.

The other half of the equation is planting seeds of thought about God, a very basic, rudimentary form of evangelism versus "preaching" relationship and sharing versus religion and "preaching." Welcome to the battle uptight church folks have dropped in our laps. Melisa had started off reading this book and just getting flat out angry at it. "This is the most negative thing I've ever read!" or "I can't believe I am leading a small group on something I don't even like," were types of comments she had about the book. She was dumbstruck that three seemingly intelligent people in our group who had finished the book sang of its praises. We talked about how as she read more her opinion changed and when something challenges your beliefs is not necessarily a bunch of garbage, but can be the catalyst to change.

This brought Bud Cox into the conversation. His gloriously Christ-like attitude about our little community, his love for it and desire to serve it, and how that can change our view of our little community. We began to reflect on how recently we'd both gotten past deep, painful hurts with our brother's, both named Mike. Mine coming as a late night birthday surprise, hers a more gradual forgiveness and healing since Christmas. How God being outside of time has the patience to slowly move in our hearts to affect change. God's relationship to time or his relationship outside of it got me thinking about how 1,000 years is like day (2 Peter 3:8), when you've got eternity you don't have to be in rush changing a persons heart.

I looked at the different stages Melisa and I had viewed Lookeba. Our view of Lookeba went from the boondocks, to the wilderness, to our place of testing; to the little town that Bud Cox loves, to a town that God loves, a place that God adores, and that God thinks is worth dying for. That's a lot of change, but it took us four years and we are in the infancy stage of living it out. I got in my mind the image of the quick-change artists that used to perform at halftime of the basketball games I'd attend at the Target Center in Minneapolis. They went through twenty outfits in the course of a four-minute song.

Here's where the almost title for this journal entry came in. I was relating to my wonder wife how marathon disc jockeys used the live version of Lynyrd Skynyrd's, Free Bird, to get naps or meals if they were running a promotion where they were staying on the air until "whatever" happened. My example was when the Baltimore Orioles started their baseball season with a long O'fer, a local DJ stayed on the air until they won a game, which was several days. Baseball, oddly enough is the pride of Lookeba, the reigning Class B Fall Baseball champions. My son, Levon having contributed to that title. See how God ties everything together? Baseball. Lookeba. Changing hearts. Changing outfits. He is incredible that way.

As we continued talking about the changing outfits topic, I asked her what outfit God was changing us into. Was it evident to others around us? Quick-change people are found in tuxedoes and flashy sequined dresses. Jesus wore a robe and sandals and washed other's feet (John 13:5). We prayed that as God changed our outfits they became more like a robe and sandals. Melisa brought to mind the passage in Isaiah about being clothed in robes of righteousness, which I thought was very cool. God wasn't done. If you go to Isaiah 61:3, it talks about planting, Isaiah 61:5 talks of farmers and pastures, Isaiah 61:10 is about God dressing us, and Isaiah 61:11 talks about the fruit of the Earth springing forth. We are so thankful that God is dressing us. If you've ever tried to dress a four year old for church or pre-school when they didn't want to be dressed, you know what a colossal hassle it can be. Our part in this is to become obedient and let God dress us how He wants to. If we do that His glory and His righteousness will be on display. It will be the most dazzling robe and sandals anyone has seen in 2,000 years. People will come up to you and say, "That's fabulous! Who's your designer?"

FEBRUARY 5ᵀᴴ
LESSONS FROM AIREDALES

The bed was awfully warm and comfortable. It called to Melisa and me to settle down and stay awhile. They say that after 21 days you form a habit. I guess that must be true because shortly after 6:00am, for reasons beyond logic, I left the snuggly heat of my bed and my wife to put on my walking clothes. Melisa, much to the credit of her character, which is substantial, got up too. There was no spiritual nudge; no holy heads up that something profound was coming. We just left the house with Dickinsonian "Great Expectations."

We weren't the only ones with expectations. Dutchess was pawing the floor of her kennel like a bull about to be released into the streets of Pamplona, and Elizabeth Taylor, usually reserved, was chatty. Thankfully her chatting was at a lower volume. Once released from their boxes, they bounded all over the living room, sometimes bumping into each other like drunken, face painted football fans celebrating a touchdown. Welcome to lesson number one. The dogs showed us that you need to be excited to be with the master. The only time these smooth tempered dogs are excited is to start their day with their masters at walk time. Luke 19:1-9 tells about a man excited to see the master and he was blessed to have the chance to have him over to dinner. The dogs exhibited an unabashed excitement and were rewarded with the desire of their heart, a long walk. Yes, my psychic abilities extend even to the canine world. Until they tell me I'm wrong, I'm going with 100% accuracy when it comes to what they are thinking or feeling.

    We get them ready for their walk by attaching their leash. We have taught them that before they get their leash, they must sit to get the reward of the leash that leads to the walk. Sitting at the feet of the master has its benefits (Luke 10:38-41). Out the door we went, ready for whatever was ahead. Down the hill past Roger's Service Station, our conversation turned to legacies. I thought what a great topic to write on today. We talked about Melisa's mother, June, who went to her eternal reward a couple of years ago, a woman with a great legacy. She outlived cancer for four years. She spoke words of hope and love to anyone who needed it in the chemo room, at church, at ballgames, without fear of what people thought.

She gave away dozens of copies of a devotional, "Prescription for a Miracle" by Mark Brazee. She credited this book with building her faith to the point where it could hold the cancer at bay.

She occasionally made her husband uncomfortable with the ease with which she slid into her testimony with total strangers. I saw this first hand in the chemo-room at Baptist Hospital in Oklahoma City. She was a bolder, braver person than me for sure. We talked about how our kids would tell their kids about the great grandma they didn't know, who was a "great" grandma, mom, wife, and witness. We prayed God would lead us to our legacy and it would bring Him glory. Our bank is Legacy Bank and I had a catchy title about investing in a legacy that you can bank on, but it wasn't meant to be.

Melisa shifted the conversation back to the dogs. How it was that they got us walking? They got us out on these walks where God reached out to us and showed us how as gentle affectionate creatures they would make great therapy dogs visiting kids in the cancer wards and the elderly. Once again it wasn't until I put the pen to the paper that I realized how God tied the legacy of June Marrow through the dogs serving the sick to the dogs showing us the lessons I feel privileged to share.

Let's go back to the beginning. This past Christmas Melisa decided to get me a dog. I'd never had a dog. The last few years I'd lived with dogs without having one of my own. Melisa and I talked about breeds and the leading candidate was the Giant Schnauzer; the hopped up on steroids version of a dog from my childhood that meets the Steve Zimmerman three rules for dogs:

1. The dog must be bigger than a football. Giants tip in at over 100 pounds.
2. They must bark, not yip; Schnauzers are breed as a guard dog, there is no question.
3. If you wrestle with them there has to be a chance no matter how small that you might lose.

We visited a couple that owned Giant Schnauzer puppies. They were cute, they were adorable, and they were $700.00. I had no peace about it. I let Melisa know of my reservation after she had sold her dog, Cooper S. Town, a tribute to America's National past time, to help defer the cost of the Giant Schnauzer. When you ruin the master plan of a planner it creates some stress. That was exactly what I did. She was upset because as a lifetime dog owner she'd sold her dog, and my brilliant and oh so sensitive suggestion was if she was going to spend $700 on a Christmas present perhaps a new TV or sofa might be a better call. That might have flown if I'd suggested it before she was dogless. After the fact, my comment was the lemon juice on her paper cut.

God was on the job. Not long after that, she found Elizabeth Taylor and Dutchess for $70.00 not $700. We got their kennels for $145 and sold Cooper for $200. A two-for-one trade (Isaiah 61:7. Yup, same Isaiah 61). When we bought them, they were not as magnificently named as they are today. The dogs we bought for one tenth of the price of a Giant Schnauzer were named Koji and Misty. It took awhile for them to adjust to their new names (Genesis 17:5; 15). It wasn't that the dogs were different it was how they were viewed by their masters. Who are you in the eyes of your Master? What is the name God calls you?

We loaded up our dogs and drove them from their nice suburban backyard in an upscale neighborhood to the 1972 mobile home in Lookeba. It took a while for them to adjust, but they are now getting regular walks, lots of love, and attention. Are you ready to adjust on the fly? Is there a better place for you where there is love and attention from a Master that wants the best for you (Genesis 12:1-3)?

We brought these outdoor, backyard dogs into our house with their new names and made them inside dogs. To begin with, inside dogs meant spending most of their time in their kennels. It was where they felt safe. It also was not where petting and hugging occurred. Eventually, when the storm of change died down, they learned to trust us and to receive the affection we had for them. Their boxes moved from a safe haven to their own little "My Space." Trusting us gave them the freedom of the whole house without costing them their own little corner of the world. Once again, giving up little returned much. I suppose I should drop a Scripture reference here and I'm sure there is one that's perfect I just don't know one. Welcome to dealing with my imperfections.

We continued training and teaching our dogs, not knowing how quickly the shoe would be on the other foot. Our dog mentor, Cesar Milan, the Dog Whisperer, often talks about the walk as the most important time. It bonds owner and dog. It establishes who the pack leader is, and in our case, walking the dogs tires them out so they don't tear up our stuff. The basic command in the walk is "heel." The heel command redirects the dog from trying to lead to resuming their proper place as follower or to walk beside. If a dog hears the "heel" command he knows he is in the company of his/her master. You are never alone when you are submitting to the heel command (Deuteronomy 31:6; Joshua 1:5; Hebrews 13:5). By allowing himself to be led, the dog is returned home safely and he gets there by being a good follower (Matthew 4:19; Matthew 8:22; John 10:4).

In the midst of the walk there are a few ways we address bad behavior, the spoken word "heel," "leave it," or with a correction with the leash, a snap or a tug. There have been times when I've been tempted to whip Dutch with the leash like we're on the homestretch at Churchill Downs on derby day. Our role model in life, God, and in dogdom, Cesar Milan, both think that is the wrong way to go about it. We've gotten excellent response from the ladies with gentle correction. By choosing to follow our correction, they get treats and kind treatment (remember being kind to the guy when buying ice at the local store in a previous journal entry?). The rewards for good following for Dutchess and Elizabeth Taylor are no different than for us (Proverbs 13:8; Proverbs 15:5; Zephaniah 3:7; Job 5:17). Everyone remembers Job as the sad sack who lost everything, "the patience of Job" and all that. Read the end of the book, He makes Donald Trump look like a hobo. There is a lot to be learned from Airedales. See you tomorrow.

February 6th
Gimme a P-R-I-D-E.
What Does it Spell?
FALL!

We are going to go in reverse this morning. For the first time since I started this project I was reluctant to write despite some amazing stuff God shared with us this morning.

Melisa, out of her enthusiasm for this project, has asked me a couple of times, "Are you gonna write today?" I bristled. I'm 40, and wife or not, I wasn't going to let her tell me what to do. She says write and I'll juggle. I don't even know how to juggle, but I'll learn so I don't do what she tells me to.

I had a choice. I could address the issue, get it out into the light and sap its power or keep that aggravation hidden in my heart until it grew big enough to blot out the joy I'd rediscovered in writing. I chose to shrivel its power by exposing it to the light. The great thing is when I asked

Melisa about it, I didn't even finish my sentence when she told me she knew and was sorry. Her response was that right after the second "You gonna to write today," was out of her mouth she regretted it. All of us, at one time or another, have clawed at the air trying to grab words that have already escaped our mouths, hoping to get them stuffed back in. Once accomplished, we swallow them so they never again see the light of day. It was so cool that she knew and it was cool when she explained that it was just her excitement getting the better of her. The truth set us free (John 8:32). I was freed from the kernel of resentment. What's so amazing about this is that by welcoming God into my day for my walks I wind up never closing the door on Him and He can keep showing me stuff after I get home. He is a God of more than I can think, hope or image (Ephesian 3:20).

Oh yeah, this is a book about dogs. Sometimes I forget. It was a morning where I thanked my lucky stars I lived in Oklahoma, and not in Minnesota. It was glorious and above all, warm. I was pretty quick to ditch the hood and unzip the jacket to stay comfortable. Melisa had done some of her end of the month paperwork and that meant sleeping in until 6:45. Whoo Hooo! It did put us into a rushed mode to get the walk in and get home in time to get the kids up for school. In a previous entry, we'd talked about how God is beyond time. He had our backs and we had exactly the right amount of time.

Out we went, loving the morning walk, with our dogs and each other. We went down the hill around the corner and past our oldest son's house. It's nice to be able to say a quick prayer over him and his new wife every morning. They don't know it, but it doesn't make it any less nice. Melisa mentioned some of the responses she'd received from emailing the first couple of days of journal entries to a select group of our friends and family. Her comments were all positive. I readily absorbed the praise. Ego's are like sponges. They take in everything and don't even feel themselves expanding.

The topic of emails got her talking about deleting forwarded emails and how much of our life were we missing because we deleted it with out looking at it. Were we deleting time with God? We looked at each other and knew we had an extra "o". It was good stuff, but it wasn't God stuff. The same bug that had bitten Melisa this morning, it just changed its name from Legacy to Deleting. She said you know that P-R-I-D-E thing? That's when I broke into the cheer that is the title for today's chapter. We realized we were trying to create a chapter so we just went straight to praying, talking to God. Prayer, oddly enough, invites a response from God that talking to each other about God just doesn't guarantee. Dutchess wants to contribute, literally sticking her nose into my business. I think she's worried about what I'm going to say about her. We started praying for our town and our families. God then decided to speak up using Melisa's mouth. It wasn't burning brush stuff, just Scripture that was our word for the day.

"If my people, who are called by my name, will HUMBLE themselves and then seek my face and turn from their wicked ways, then I will hear them from heaven and will forgive their sins and heal their land" (2 Chronicles 7:14).

Normally I don't write out Scripture, but having no memory of that Scripture (even though it's underlined in my Bible), please refer to Joshua 1:8 (also underlined in my Bible). I was wowed by how much of that Scripture played out. Our prideful behavior was addressed in the first line. Once again we were trying to show how insightful we were, how deep we could get, instead of letting God say what He wanted to through us. The way to get the right insight for writing was to pray. The sin forgiven was pride. It is the last line in that passage I love the best. While walking the land and praying for the land, the healing was addressed. I've celebrated a healing of sorts with my brother, not a Benny Hinn, slap you in the forehead kind of healing, but healing nonetheless. I've long held a belief that the Bible is a series of if this, then that promises. "If you pray and seek My face, then I will heal the land".

Scripture coming alive! That's why they call it the "Living Word" or the "Living Water."

I got an idea when thinking about the phrase "the land" just now. My father-in-law, Gene Marrow, has a large piece of land we affectionately refer to as "the farm." He has an aerial photo of his land that shows how large it is. Behind his house is a lake he built. Its 30 feet deep and he has a picture of him at the bottom of the lake with a pillar of pipe that goes up to what is now the surface. These two examples of "the land" keep things in perspective, reminding us how small we can be. The land keeping us humble so it can be healed and we can avoid taking a fall.

February 7th
"Whistling Dixie"

We headed out this morning and were immediately faced with an unexpected challenge. One we thought was a sure fire topic for today's entry. We have an "adopted" son named Cory Bare, who is one of Levon's best friends. He eats at our house a lot and says Melisa's chili is his favorite meal. We've even taken him to Minnesota with us over spring break. His dog, once the proud property of our oldest son, Mark, is named Dixie. Dixie is a town dog, meaning she runs the town pretty much at her leisure when she is out. My city sensibilities go bonkers at the idea of exercising no control over your dogs, but it's a fact of life here in Lookeba. We are the exception in that we walk our dogs on leashes.

Here we come, civilized and dignified, walking our dogs on leashes and over the hill comes Dixie, bouncing along encouraging our dogs to frolic when it is not frolicking time. Dutchess starts pulling on her leash and spinning in circles trying to play with Dixie. If our dogs were trained to the point where they would come when called and I wasn't worried about being late for work, an impromptu play session might be in order. This was not the case. After some pretty severe lead corrections, including having to put Dutchess in "time out" which is a sit/stay, (to restore the mindset of receiving and obeying commands) order was restored. This didn't prevent Dixie, a Walker Coon dog, from flitting around the periphery of our walk like a large unwanted firefly.

  We began talking about distractions, and how the devil uses them to get us away from doing what God had planned. Notice the devil doesn't get to come up with anything original. He just gets to go against whatever God wants. Even "original" sin wasn't original. It was just the negative of what God said (Genesis 3:1-6). Was Dixie a God sent living symbolism of distractions and temptations? As she circled back for what seemed her 19th pass around the five of us, Melisa mentioned that if you defeat temptation, it will no doubt come around again. Ask Robert Downy Jr. when he leaves whatever rehab center Lindsey Lohan is recommending this month. What did this loveable lout of a dog have to say to us from the throne room of God? The answer...drum role please...NOTHING! The discussion came and went and my spirit felt nothing about Dixie being a word from God.

I was a little crest fallen. It looked like a perfect set up. Alas it wasn't to be. What if God didn't say anything? This inspiring project had injected so much joy into my pen and my life, would it come to a screeching halt? Of course not. What do you leave when walking? Footprints. How many of us have seen the poem, "Footprints" on a poster, bookmark or plaque? It's about God being there when you don't know it; faith in His presence, whether you sense Him or not. BINGO!! This bubbled to the top of our consciousness and I started singing, "Walk By Faith" by Jeremy Camp. Thank you, God! I use the term singing in its loosest possible meaning. It sounds better than warbling and takes up less ink than making a joyful noise. Needless to say they won't even let me on American Idol. I sang of faith and we prayed about faith and faith increased our ability to hear from God. My faith calmed me down as I had gotten a little upset with Dutchess' antsy behavior. My faith and the peace it generated knowing a fifth and most important traveling partner was there, albeit quiet, traveled down the leash. Dutchess settled down when I settled down. Pack leader setting the tone for the follower. My increased faith allowed me to hear God's voice. Ever the gentleman, He refused to shout. It gave me the heightened hearing that allows dogs to hear dog whistles.

Walking With God

Melisa and I finally got the message and were once again thrilled by God's faithfulness to talk to us. No wet blanket, He was willing to participate, as He is every morning, He just wasn't going to make a spectacle of Himself to get our attention. We were so thankful that He never wants to be away from us, that He wants an all day dialogue (Ephesians 6:18). We were filled with joy as we headed into the homestretch (Nehemiah 8:10). Dixie had one more parting shot for us. We were heading up Main Street when from out of nowhere came Dixie, head high, tail high. Any good dog behaviorist worth his salt will tell you head high, tail high is a happy dog. Then I heard in my heart, "Be a Dixie" choose joy and sow joy. So I did.

February 8th
Heads or Tails?
We Get to Call it in the Air

I spoke yesterday about leaving the doors open so God could talk to me after I get home from my walk. He seized the opportunity to start talking before we got out of bed. Technically, I suppose, He started last night before we even got home.

Wednesday night Bud Cox had a showing of the movie "Facing the Giants," to which Melisa gave an enthusiastic two thumbs up. I was coming home from church in the city, and I noticed the cars were still at the church. I did a little Carpe Diem action and decided it was the time to introduce myself to the man: the myth, the legend, Bud Cox. He doesn't even know he is any of these things yet, but it's only a matter of time. I met him and wow, Melisa hadn't sold him short. The waves of energy and joy he emitted were undeniable. He is the human Red Bull. Just drink him in.

    This morning we began talking about Levon and his future and how amazing it would be if there was a revival with the high school baseball team. Levon would be able to flourish into the leader we know he can become. Ballparks can be like dog parks where the pack, especially the pack leader will institute conformity. A dog will be pushed and pressured into adopting the attitude and energy of the pack. We talked about how hard it can be to change an established culture. Sometimes it seemed like it would take a miracle to pull something like that off. We are fortunate that we walk daily with a God who still traffics in miracles (Hebrews 13:8).

    Out we went walking down the hill as our conversation meandered. We began talking about Renee who goes to Bud's church. She lives next door to our adopted senior citizen, Ada Franks. Renee has found a home at Bud's church at the right time as she is going though a rough spell in her life. We began thinking of creative ways in which Renee could earn some extra money. Melisa said that Renee made these large elaborate collages "to pass the time" as she put it. They are themed by decades. We talked about having her do other themes like baseball or OU and seeing if she could sell them.

    This fired another pinball into my brain to ricochet around. Collage turned to mosaic, mosaic to pointillism.

Similar schools of art making a bigger picture out of lots of little pieces. That is exactly what God is doing with us. Connecting a couple of points everyday. As the days pile up so do the dots and slowly, but surely the picture of life God wants us to lead is made clear. The other thing that came to the forefront in regards to Renee was to try to show her she had a talent. If we can show her she has value, gifts, and talents, we can be used by God to help shift her paradigm. You get people into relationship with God and out of religion when you show them they have value to God and reflect that value in how you treat them.

Radically loving others like God does will make you stand out. There are many examples of people God used who stood out and how being used caused them to stand out. Noah came to mind. Want to set yourself up for a hard time? Build a huge ship when it had never rained. In the New International Version it talks about all the "crap" Noah took from people. Standing up for God doesn't go unnoticed (James 1:2-5; 1 Corinthians 4:12; Matthew 5:10). God pays you back in spades for any grief you take on His behalf.

Keeping with the ark idea, there are not a lot of places in the Bible where God gives us specific directions and specific dimensions. For the good of all readerdom's spiritual health, you need to listen to Bill Cosby's routine on Noah to understand what a cubit is and why it was important to Noah. God told him exactly how big to make the ark. God has exact plans for us. How well we listen and follow instruction is up to us (Jeremiah 29:11). The ark designed by God to function perfectly. The Ford Pinto (my wife's first new car) designed by man, not so good. The ark designed by God to save humanity was perfect. The Titanic designed by man, to pamper man, less successful. Granted, one boat had a live band (please track down and listen to "Dance Band on the Titanic," by Harry Chapin) and good food, while the other had every kind of animal crap known to man. Our best choice isn't always the most appealing. One plan is God's, one plan is man's and we get to choose (Deuteronomy 5:26-29; Deuteronomy 30:19). God lays it out for us and gets out of the way so our free choice rules the day. The ark or the Titanic, heads or tails, call it in the air.

February 9th
More than Meets the Eye

We went out en masse this morning; all four dogs, Melisa and I. Informed last night about cold weather and the possibility of freezing fog, we boldly ventured forth. Not knowing what was in store, but ready to receive it. Blessed by weather once again, it was not as scary as predicted. Melisa said as we took our right turn past Mark and Brianna's house towards the bridge God's presence showed up she wanted to close her eyes and take all of it in. We fully intend to have our dogs trained as therapy dogs, but not Seeing Eye Dogs. The road is wide enough and it's hardly as if we're strolling into the heart of Lookeba rush hour. We began talking about what our eyes take in. When I look at that topic now I think about common phrases, such as about seeing "more than meets the eye," "turn a blind eye," "blink and you will miss it," and "looks can be deceiving." A lot of these sayings indicated that our eyes are not our most reliable source of information. For people, I think our most reliable source is our hearts. I have no rock solid scientific evidence to back that up. Our friends, Dutchess and Elizabeth Taylor, trusted their ears and noses for the first week or so of life before they even opened their eyes.

    Melisa punctuated this point by recalling a scene from "Facing the Giants" where one of the team leaders is asked to crawl 20 yards with a teammate on his back. Before the coach starts the exercise he asked the player to promise to hold nothing back. "This time you have to give me your all," the coach said. This brought to mind how Jesus lived and more importantly how he died. Hanging on the cross He spoke to the thieves hanging with him. Some of his last words were an utterance of prayer. That's what I call putting in a full day's life, knowing you won't get to take advantage of the overtime on your last paycheck. How many of us in our last moments alive get to save a soul and redeem mankind. Ok, I give. It may be unrealistic to expect Christ-like results for our final seconds on planet Earth, but yeah we're young. We've got the rest of our lives to build our body of work. So let's start today (as I stealthily lead it back to football). I'll put down my pompoms. Back to "Facing the Giants," the coach takes this star player and blindfolds him. Without his sight feeding him information about what he can and can't do, this kid crawls the length of the field with just his coach's voice, his heart, his muscles, and a promise to give his all to inspire him. He in turn inspires his teammates and hopefully us.

Listen to the coach in the sky, one of the many names of God. I'm 100% sure that one doesn't appear in the Bible. Oh well. ☺ Listen to Him. Give Him 100% and you'll be amazed at what the two of you can do together. You won't believe your eyes.

FEBRUARY 10ᵀᴴ
WARTS AND ALL

You can't write a book about dogs without addressing the age-old debate. There are many great debates throughout time. In many of these, passions run high and fence sitting is not allowed: Yankees/Red Sox, Marx brothers/Three Stooges, Star Wars/Star Trek, or squeezing the toothpaste from the bottom or the middle? I will not stake my claim in any of those, but when it comes to dogs versus cats, my voice must be heard. I have been in the dog corner since being attacked by a cat while I was collecting for my paper route when I was 13; clawing, hissing, jumping, fur on it's back raised up, the whole nine yards. Did the owner thump it or even discipline it? Of course not.

  Cats are the baby sisters of the pet world; spoiled, pampered, allowed to get away with completely everything and they are completely oblivious to the needs of others. I hoped to keep this from becoming a cat bashing session, but I guess the cat is out of the bag. I'd have been better off if the cat had my tongue. Even the sayings about cats aren't good things. I prefer the cat in the bag in the river, but I don't get to make the rules. On the other hand, dogs are loyal, affectionate (to a fault sometimes), trainable (ever heard of a Seeing Eye Cat?), and they love unconditionally. I have only bonded with Dutchess for a bit more than a month, but if I sit on the floor treats are not necessary for her to come and lay her head on my leg for some lovins.

Dogs don't need drugs to be happy; "dog nip" doesn't exist. My Dutchess is thrilled to see me in the morning and after her breakfast she is more than happy to push my pen along with her nose when I'm doing my scribing, recording the days events and reflections. They love like God, perfectly and without end. In Nicholas Sparks's book, "The Guardian," the dog takes a bullet for the owner, a willing sacrifice, so that his owner could live. In God's book, the Bible, Jesus took the nails that we might have everlasting life. That is the supernatural love I am talking about. I am almost as late to the world of parenting as I am to dog owning. I have three wonderful, unique kids who have blessed my life. I am blessed and honored to be their bonus dad. I'm a bonus dad because steps are something that gets walked on and bonus is something in addition to. I love my kids and I'm not sure there is anyone out there reading my words for which I'd sacrifice them. I am so grateful that God's love is greater than mine. God loves us warts and all.

Here are some warts. My lovely wife and I are past the midway point in today's walk when the subject of 'wants' arises. I express that I don't often feel like I get to act on my wants. She asked for an example. This causes me to think this is going to become God-ordained conversation that will propel our marriage to a high level of trust and openness. I let her know that I was aware that she felt I wasn't home enough. I work in Oklahoma City and drive over an hour one way. My new schedule, thanks to a lateral promotion, pushed my late days even later. I am a city person. I like malls and Starbucks. I even like traffic in moderation. Sometimes I want to stay in the city and shop. I told her I don't because I know she feels I'm gone too much.

I am expecting gratitude and appreciation for my openness and my considering her feelings. What I got was a cup of cold water thrown in my face. Much to my surprise, I'm informed how my martyr act is getting tiresome.

Do I take this in stride? I don't, I feel myself snap into a defensive posture and button down my emotions, cold and precise. I choose my words with sterile precision. My argument cannot be nit picked because of language nor any phrase misunderstood. It's a chance for me to be summer school teacher correcting the bad student. Cold, methodical and most importantly heartless, that's how I fight back. A half a mile of he said/she said not corrections made out of love, but accusations made out of pain. This is punctuated with Melisa laying down this challenge, "Put that in your journal and make it look pretty." Having chewed that over most of the day I decided not to.

Eventually calmer heads prevailed. Apologies were said. I went back to dogs and God and the right way to love people. The Dog Whisperer says, "Dogs live in the now, so they don't forgive, they forget." God lives outside of time and He's all about forgiveness (1 John 1:9; Micah 7:19). My wife's mantra for her Christian life is, "It's all about your love walk." Mine is, "Being a Christian means to follow Christ." Put them together and you've got a call to love as much like God as possible (Matthew 22:37-39). We won't get it right all the time. We are going to take this morning's lesson about forgiveness and use it to get better. Love a little bit more like God next time. So until next time...

FEBRUARY 12ᵀᴴ
I'M NOT CHARLES BARKLEY

Sometimes I remember the genesis of our conversations and at other times I don't. Today would fall into the latter category. By hook or by crook or by God the topic came around to role models. Whammo, I just remembered! I guess turning 40 is over rated as far as being over the hill. We were talking about our pastor, Mark Crow and our friend Pastor Bud Cox, and how they didn't care what other people thought about them, but they were only concerned about what God thought about them. You handle getting right with God and the rest just falls into place. From there I leapfrogged to the fact that they are role models. There is no one like Pastor Mark. He inspires people through his leadership. We as parents are role models whether we want to be or not. I wonder about my leadership ability because I often feel like the kids don't follow me. The flip side is at church, there are several people who sign up for every small group Melisa and I lead due to our leadership style. At work I have several protégés who come to me with questions and me first. It is probably that my leadership is better suited to adults. That is perhaps why I chose to marry a woman with three kids opposed to infants or toddlers.

Parenting and leadership is not the same thing, neither are parenting and role modeling. The act of walking your dog establishes you as the pack leader as you dictate pace, distance, and behavior to your dog. You give commands and corrections to your dog. The dog that gets the affection and treats (rewards) is the dog that learns to heel, yield, and submit to his/her master Luke 22:47; Mark 14:36; Matthew 26:39).

Melisa and I talked further about our two youngest wanting to live with their dad. How much we wanted them to choose us first. With our oldest, it's not so much his dad as it is his in-laws over us. In an effort to invest in our kids, we've dedicated Sunday night to them and that has met with mixed results. Despite giving them control over the dinner menu and the social planning. We began looking at this and the phrase that kept coming to mind was "pick me." The problem with that is the focus is a "me" mindset. It needs to be turned inside out to "I love you."

My mom, a very wise and modest woman, has told me several times she didn't like her four kids very much between the ages of 15 and 25, but we are some of her best friends now. You try to raise your children so that what you sow into them gives a harvest in adulthood. I'm impatient; I want to see my harvest now from our teenagers. Can you tell I've only been doing this parent thing for a few years? I want my kids joyfully singing the refrain from Bill Cosby's parenthood, "Dad is great, he gives us the chocolate cake." Not appropriate for breakfast, but a great way to curry favor with kids, not a good seed to sow. It was decided we would have to trust that things would change.

This took the conversation to a different track. If we can trust God in our finances, why can't we trust Him to grow our relationship with our kids? Is it because our God isn't big enough or is it because our faith is too small? With a dog, once it becomes your dog it will always chose you. Kids have more free will and a whole lot more independence. We need to plant seeds of obedience in our kids (as well as our dogs) and give them time to root. If we keep messing with seeds that are planted then roots will not develop (Genesis 8:22). Dogs require a lot more watering and tending and your harvest is lot more limited. A dog does however; provide a great deal of his own fertilizer.

Back to the point of this section, how big is our God? We have this idea that we are being wonderfully mature Christians that gives us an advantage (1 Corinthians 3:2; Hebrews 5:12). However, we haven't even trusted God in our relationship with our kids. We don't have an incomplete God, but rather we have an immature faith. I'm hoping what I share on these pages allows us all to grow up a bit together.

February 13th
Canceled on Account of Mud

We didn't walk today because with all the rain our driveway is a mud bog and the dogs, not to mention ourselves, will track it into the house. I read Melisa what I wrote for yesterday. I asked her if she thought I got too personal. She then laid some wisdom on me, "People don't learn too much from people who are perfect." I took that and thought how discouraging it might be to hear how perfect we were and have nothing to apply to the lives of others. Welcome to our anger, insecurities, doubts, and shortcomings. The wonderful thing about our imperfection is it gives us a goal (Matthew 5:48). There is also a promise that in some aspects of our lives is attainable. It sounds amazing, but check out Hebrews 10:14 and James 1:4. This entry is short, but I hope you liked it.

February 14th
The Power of Three

The number three has always been my favorite number. I wore it on my baseball uniform as a kid and if I couldn't get 3, I'd get 3 +3 or 3 x 3. I was the third child born on the third day of February. My memory is a little foggy about that day 40 years ago, but if it serves, it was about three in the morning and was probably around 13 degrees outside. Ok I made that last part up. If you're dying for details, you can ask my mom. The point is I've always loved the number three. So does God. It has a special place, Father, Son, and Holy Spirit. It is referred to as the number of completion.

My wife and I talked this morning about a Bible study she had written. It's the same Bible study that we had talked about with Bud and Paula Cox at breakfast on Monday. They had invited her to share it with their small congregation later this evening. She had written this a couple of years ago. The initial voyage was with a couple of friends in our home. That lasted a couple of weeks then died out. To the shelf it went for months, dutifully holding its spot until its appointed time. It was revived at a small local church only to be swallowed up in a storm of controversy, bureaucracy and religion. From the church to the house owned by the church to the living room of a woman from the church it went. Another short run and the same results were achieved.

We talked about what was different this time and decided most importantly our hearts were. Our hearts for other people had been re-awakened. The second thing was this would be God's Word, in God's house with the backing of a man of God. We decided this was a trifecta that would lead to greater results. This just shows you should never give up. God's time is different than ours. Patience and faith will bring whatever He has for you to fruition. I kept hearing the late North Carolina State basketball coach, Jim Vulvano telling anyone who would listen during his fight with cancer, "Don't give up, don't ever give up." You've heard it since you were a kid, but it doesn't make it any less true.

God was busy this morning. It was as if He had his Polaroid camera of really cool divine knowledge with him today. I thought I'd share a few of His snapshots with you. We have made a point of praying for our town and the houses we walk by whether we know who lives there or not. We were walking, enjoying the company and I just got this picture in my head of a huge God-cloud rolling in. It broke into pieces and settled on the roofs of the houses and just melted into the homes.

Melisa got the next one. As we were passing a streetlight, she noticed our shadows. There was a darker primary shadow and a brighter secondary one as if there was double vision in the shadow world. Psalm 91 talks about the shadow of the Most High. We've always felt Him while we walked, but now we've seen it, very cool. We've talked about seeing God in the big things and in the little things. Melisa called it having HD God glasses. Here's what I'm talking about. We've had a lot of rain recently. Please refer to February 13th journal entry. Our driveway has a gathering place for excess water, more commonly referred to as a puddle. In this case a small pond is almost in reach. The pond has a thin sheet of ice this morning in the 10-degree heat. The ice was thin. The tax collector walking on it was not. When you are on thin ice and you could go through, 2.2 miles in a right shoe-sopping wet with 10-degree weather might have hastened an early cancellation. God had my back and for some reason the ice cracked all over, but held my weight and the walk was saved. HD God glasses seeing God in a little thing.

Melisa passed up two for one bags of Starbucks coffee yesterday. Normally it's a sure sign of insanity, but not when the still small voice is telling you not to buy it, you obey. Upon further review, the expiration date on the coffee says best if sold by May 2006. Thank God we see Him in the little things and say, 'thanks'. Thanksgiving is not just a holiday anymore. Make it an everyday thing and you'll be better for it. That's the desire of God for us to be a little better every day. Be a little more like Him every day. So let's get in agreement and make it happen.

February 15th
What's Your Passion?

We spent the majority of our walk praying for a local youth pastor who strayed in a pretty substantial way. He left his wife, his job, and his calling. We all have free will. God doesn't tie us down to a lifestyle or any decision. The youth pastor just made the decision to bolt. A few days back, Dutchess and Elizabeth Taylor dug their way out of their pen and were startled by their freedom. Having known so little of it for so little time, they didn't know what to do, so they ran. It was Levon and Cory's job to drive all over town to try to bring them back home. I was at work and missed the whole episode. The boys were unhappy, but to the best of my knowledge they didn't beat the dogs. Melisa was so happy to see them back. That's how God feels about this anointed youth pastor. God has big plans for him (Matthew 18:12-14; Luke 15:4-7). We welcomed home the dogs. He will be welcomed home too.

Walking With God

There will be a ripple effect through - Caring Hearts Church, Levon Lumpkin, and the area as things are set right - a three-fold ripple effect.

One of the other topics we touched on was hobbies and passions. I have a passion for small groups, but I could hardly call it a hobby. Bud's passion is the lost people, at least being given a chance to choose God. This is also the passion of Mark Crow, the Pastor at Victory Church. Where does this fit in with Melisa and me? It was neither a passion nor a hobby. We just gave it to God so He could make it the priority He feels it needs to be in our lives.

Melisa asked me if I was prepared to stay in Lookeba. I was a little thrown by this question. We had always talked about being able to get out of debt so if we were called to move we could pack up and go. I'd never considered staying. If God can move us anywhere then he can keep us here. He is a God of everything and anything. There is a song by Steven Curtis Chapman called, "Anything" that talks about how you shouldn't try to out think God (Proverbs 3:5; Isaiah 55:8). Trust in His decisions and let yourself be led and let faith develop (Hebrews 11:1-2). We walked today like every other day. Today was different. It was about six degrees outside. Eventually I stopped feeling my nose. I couldn't smell. Just because I couldn't feel my nose or I couldn't see it, doesn't mean it

Steven Zimmerman

wasn't there. Like the wind or God, I take it on faith that they're there. The deciding factor was my glasses didn't fall off my face so they must have been resting on something, unless of course they had frozen to the sides of my head. Glad to report I'm inside, thawed out, and present and accounted for, nose and all.

February 16th
Be Vewwy Qwiet

Our walk began uneventfully enough, but that changed before we left our driveway. Out from our left side darted a rabbit. The dogs went nuts. Terriers are bred for tracking game and game close to the ground. Every instinct in their bodies said chase. We didn't let them. Melisa busted out some dog owner kung fu and had Elizabeth Taylor in a very aggressively attained down/stay. Order was quickly restored and we were a lot more aware for a few blocks, not wanting a repeat of the Dixie experience. Her correction was as harsh as I've seen her with Elizabeth Taylor. Once done and everything calmed down, we both noticed and commented that Melisa had refused to surrender her joy to the sudden chaos. Oddly enough Elizabeth Taylor took on the same countenance. A harsh rebuke, but she didn't hang her head or leave her tail between her legs. Dogs live in the now and joy was quickly restored to

Steven Zimmerman

Elizabeth Taylor's stride.

We started throwing back and forth some of our standard points of view; joy is a choice, sow joy reap joy, the joy of the Lord is my strength (Nehemiah 8:10). We got to thinking about the origins of our joy. If my joy is from my bonus check or my car, once my bonus check gets spent and my car breaks down then where will I be? The converse of that is if my joy comes from an eternal source (Revelation 1:8) like God our joy isn't fleeting. Temporal source equals temporal joy. Eternal source equals eternal joy.

We marched along praying over the town. Pastor Mark Crow has taken to using the term occupying the territory until Jesus comes. Marching and occupying are both military terms. My brother had a brief flirtation with the military and my oldest son, Mark, is currently serving in the National Guard. The idea of us as soldiers in the Lord's army came into play. Good soldiers follow orders. Good soldiers who follow orders get promoted. They don't write their own orders, but take them from high up. The last couple of days have created some stress because we were trying to divine our orders for two years from now or five years from now. We became soldiers getting out of line and getting into strife. Soldiers don't determine where they are stationed, or else every one would be stationed at Pearl Harbor or in San Diego. Some of us are "stationed" in Lookeba and some in more metropolitan locals. Okay, short of Borneo, most places are more metropolitan. The point is soldiers go where they are stationed and bust their butts wherever that is until further notice.

We felt we were told we would be in Lookeba five years. We were not told anything past that. If we get another five years here, it's our job to live a life filled with joy that draws others to God (Matthew 5:14). If it is the city then it is the city with our whole heart and best effort. The soldier's ultimate goal is victory. Our commanding officer has already secured it (Revelation 1:18). That is the kind of army I wish Mark served in, one in which victory was already in hand.

Mark makes me so proud. It's hard enough to serve in the military in peacetime, but to sign up when terms like Vietnam and quagmire are flying around takes a particular courage. He has never backed down. He has also maintained his ability to be his own man. I just can't write about soldiers without bragging about the wild kid who is now a soldier, a husband, and an amazing source of pride to his bonus dad. I salute you Mark Lumpkin Jr.

February 17th
Canceled on Account of Service

I have to admit, I never pictured myself a dog owner. We only had dogs for a couple of weeks as a kid. My father, the lawyer drew up a contract for the kids to sign about caring for, feeding and potty duties. As kids, we failed miserably and the dog's stay with us was short. My mother lives in the same house, dog free to this day. Today, dogs of all shapes, sizes, and colors surround me. I moved from living with dogs to owning one. I find myself growing fonder of Dutchess every day. Dutchess doesn't have, nor will she ever have, any doggie sweaters, doggie booties or any doggie clothing. DOGS ARE NOT PEOPLE! They should never be elevated above people.

Friends of ours are moving this morning. We are going to help them. We choose to give our time to people rather than the dogs. This is not as altruistic as it sounds. It did allow us to sleep in and actually sit down for breakfast. Dogs are wonderful. They teach you more than you realize. People are better. It's all about relationships. That's what comes out at your funeral. Grow your vertical relationship with God and your horizontal relationships with as many people as possible. People are roots and the more roots established, the more wind the tree can withstand. Grow your roots even if your dog doesn't approve.

February 18th
Goats and Sheep

This journal started out as a way to remember things that came up on our walks. We bounced it off our friends Michael and Angela Delk. It got two thumbs up and the mass email was spawned. We both have been guilty of trying to dictate the day's topic. The first few days were lightening bolts from the sky. The next few, Melisa and I created so much thunder it was hard to distinguish God's voice from our own noise. Today it took a while to get through the noise. Sometimes these things are dissertations and some times they are bullet points. One of these bullet points came to me as I crested the hill past the Johnston's longhorns. I looked to my right and saw land and nothing, but land. I looked to my left and saw the same thing (Genesis 13:14-15).

  We made the turn and headed back, hanging a left at the Missionary Baptist Church. Did it ever dawn on anyone that Missionary Baptist Church would be empty because everyone was in the mission field? We get to the little farm in town. They have two dogs that run the fence trying to convince our dogs to help them escape from Stalag 13. Anyone who's seen any episodes of Hogan's Heroes knows there's never been a successful escape under the Colonel Klink regime. Across the road are the cows, goats and about four or five donkeys. The goats and the donkeys are the least glamorous of the barnyard animals; even the pigs have Babe and Charlotte's web. Other than the Shrek series, name the last good goat or donkey movie you've seen.

It was just brought to mind of the Sermon on the Mount (Matthew 5). God's is the kingdom in reverse. The least shall be first. Who are the donkeys and goats of the world? Are we treating the least as the first? There is a line from a song by Todd Agnew called, "My Jesus" that says "Jesus probably wouldn't be welcome in my church. The blood and the dirt might stain the carpet." Who are we missing out on? FM Static has a song called, "Crazy Mary" that talks of what might change for a street person who was loved.

Why is God better than us? He loves the least first and He loves who's in first, all the while not neglecting the middle. He loves us all the best everyday.

We are going to shift to a more canine gear. On the

way home we tried a little experiment. How many of you know that experiments don't always give accurate results until they have been repeated. Melisa let Elizabeth Taylor off her leash, she wandered six to ten feet away when Melisa called her and she came right back and there was much rejoicing. She let her go again with the same results. It was a triumphant moment for us as dog owners. Now it was Dutchess' turn. We re-leashed Elizabeth Taylor. Two loose dogs at the same time would be disastrous! An amazing thing happened. Dutchess walked beside me. No leash. It was cool. She walked back to see her sister, then came right back to me. We were very proud of our dogs. I looked around and didn't see the worm that was about to turn.

It got even better. We went off to dog class. Dutchess was wonderful, an A+ student. I encourage everyone to take their dog to dog school or sit in on a class and bring the teaching home. We went from class to pick up Melisa at her cousin's home. She has been at a Pampered Chef party while I was in dog class. Dutchess was fresh out of class and on her best behavior. She came in and performed a sit/stay despite our friend Steve reaching out to pet her. Steve looked at me oddly with a look that said, 'why she doesn't like me.' I told him I'd given her a command, "stay" and hadn't released her yet. We have a release word, "now." I gave her the release word

Walking With God

and she went straight to him for some lovins. My kids are not my birth kids. I missed out on their first everything, except maybe their first speeding ticket. I'm still proud of them. My dog is mine and I was very proud of her today. Live a life that says I've been to obedience school and make your Father proud.

February 19th
The Worm

Our walk today didn't come with profound revelations. If there were profound revelations, I've forgotten, and to everyone's detriment. After our walk Sunday we had hustled through our morning and headed church. We had Elizabeth Taylor in tow. She was heading off to PetSmart for her first ever grooming, another first for one of the "new" kids. You remember just earlier that morning we had let her off her leash twice and she had returned to Melisa both times without any problems. Melisa accidentally dropped the leash. Out of the ground, thundering like a herd of buffalo came the worm. It turned viciously and as it turned so did Elizabeth Taylor. She turned and ran. She ran fast and she ran away. We called, she ran. We acted excited, she ran. Eventually we ran to our cars to chase her.

I found myself singing part of a children's song

Melisa had taught me, "The joy of the Lord is my strength," sung and whistled at various cadences. During this situation, something as simple as a children's song helped me in eminent Christian maturity. It allowed me to keep my cool and go on to a fabulous day. We crisscrossed town with no luck. Melisa heard in her spirit to go home, where she found Levon with Elizabeth Taylor at the front door. She asked him with great trepidation, "Did you beat her?" "Not yet," was his reply through clenched teeth. Elizabeth Taylor very peacefully loaded in the car off to PetSmart. We were able to enjoy small group, church, lunch with our friends, unhindered by the trials of the morning. We also got to enjoy the new made-over and regal looking Elizabeth Taylor without wanting to clock her.

February 20th
Walking Blind

I was awfully quiet this morning. It wasn't so much that I was busy listening to what God was saying to me as much as it was enjoying what He was sharing with me. I just had an awesome peace. It was the kind of peace a VW bus full of hippies would kill for (Philippians 4:7). I luxuriated in it.

Our goal for the dogs, are for them to eventually become therapy dogs. Our goal has never been for them to be Seeing Eye Dogs. I was so peaceful, so certain that God was with me that I just closed my eyes. Dutchess led me and my feet never left the road. I gave Dutchess to Melisa and closed my eyes with the same result. It was the unique feeling that if it could be bottled would have ended my career as a tax collector and magnified my role as a taxpayer. I was wonderfully reminded that time with God is always time well spent, whether it's about talking to God or not. It may even be the beauty of a pink-purple sunset, my wife's favorite color. She never forgets to thank God when she sees one. Whatever you're doing, it is worth the investment.

When I decided to join the conversation, we talked about the sermon on Sunday. The junior high pastor who is almost young enough to be my son talked about getting back to our "first love." Melisa and I used to do Bible study over the phone every night when we lived 900 miles apart. It was a given, whether it was 9pm, midnight or 2am, it got done. It has sort of fallen by the wayside from time to time. We used to talk excitedly about how amazing it would be when we were in the same room. We both felt like we'd let God down. That's a pretty ugly feeling. You died on the cross for me and I can't even give you a little reading every night. You know what, that had become our idea of what we should do to "be with God." Time with God is what being in a relationship is about. It doesn't matter what we do with Him; 30 minutes studying Philemon or 30 minutes talking to Him while walking our dogs, it doesn't matter to Him. God showed us that what was important was being with Him.

We mulled this over and we starting making lists about what we were doing and what could be dropped to wedge in this mandatory Bible study. There were cuts to be made, sacrificed to the name of what is the "right" way to spend time with God. We looked at what we were doing and our time with God is many-fold. It was Melisa preaching, our small group, our walks, and this journal. All were good and all were God things, and we almost talked ourselves out of these activities. My point is not to give a laundry list of our great deeds, but to show how God can be in all sorts of things we do. It helps the relationship live (James 2:26).

We left a little earlier and worked some obedience class training into our walk. Our dogs get trained together, apart, alone, and with distractions. Our commitment to training is going to lead to excellence. A commitment to living an excellent life will lead to hearing, "Well done my good and faithful servant" (Matthew 25:21).

Melisa ran with the dogs for a bit today. We both get winded, but we share the duty. The dogs both love it. I'm sure if we took a bicycle they would run the whole 2.2 miles. Sharing the running is like sharing the dishes or the laundry. We both work with each other's dog. We employ the same rules and boundaries (Ecclesiastes 4:12). Bringing God into everything makes everything easier. We finished our walk going up a good size hill. It is always easier when we have a lot of God giving us momentum. One of the first small groups we led was called, "Doing Life Together." Live, do and invite God along for the ride. He just might surprise you and do most of the heavy lifting for you.

February 21ˢᵀ
40 Times

G-O-R-geous!!! The last two days started out at 45 degrees on their way to 70+. Oklahoma can be a wonderful place to be.

On Sunday we had a small group leaders meeting. The topic was what is in your heart and what are you connecting to. Melisa talked about her primary love language, acts of service. Could it be motivated by being plugged into a bad self image in her heart? Was she trying to compensate? She really had been giving it some intensive thought. I concluded that it was good that days after the meeting it was still food for thought. We needed food to grow physically, mentally, and spiritually. If my mind expands like my waistline I will be a very wise old man. Dogs seem to eat at one of two speeds; either they wolf it down like it's there last meal or a leisurely nibble here and nibble there. Gertie, my daughter's dog, takes a couple of pieces of food from her bowl, walks into the living room and chews it and swallows it. Chewing is under-rated. People and dogs need to value it.

As a child I was told we were supposed to chew each bite 40 times before swallowing. It would prevent us from choking. If you got a dog from the last meal school, you know that chewing is optional. The result of that is occasionally a big, steaming pile of dog vomit. The bad part is they never clean up after themselves, but at least you get a good idea of what they had for dinner (1 Corinthians 3:2; Hebrews 5:12; 1 Peter 2:2). The point is we had to chew on this because it is substantial and substantial is good. It challenged Melisa and she accepted the challenge. Seeing that she was maybe plugged into a negative thought pattern in her heart, she has aggressively looked at her heart and I'm willing to bet there is going to be an incredible change for the better.

Don't back down from meat, even if you have to chew on it for days, weeks, or months. I say order up steaks all around. Meat, it's what's for dinner.

February 22ND
Obedience School - It's for All of Us

Another day, another 2.2 miles and our blessed weather pattern continued. Switched to the light suede jacket and shelved the down jackets.

We started talking about religion and religiousness and how it soaks into us often through the church we attend. The God you know is often introduced to you by the church you attend. The question was posed, "What kind of God do you know?" Is He a mad and angry God all about smiting people? God is pretty much the only one in the smiting business. I think about a song by Dar Williams called, "Teen for God," which talks about college kids needing a God for such cynical times. Many people have an antiseptic, distant God. What kind of God do you know? Melisa and I agreed we both knew a good, kind God overflowing with love for His children. This begged the question, how do we introduce God to those who don't know any God or know a different God? Sermon Alert! Sermon Alert! (Insert loud siren and drum noise here!). The way you show people your God is done in 3 ways:

> 1. Know the Scriptures. They are the most in depth description of God and the character of God. You know his character, you know Him. He is the same yesterday, today and tomorrow. It's His autobiography and diary.
> 2. Show God's love. Talk is cheap. Actions speak louder than words. Jesus talked about loving one another and said upon this rests all the other law and the prophets. Loving correctly is what melts the chains of hypocrites from the pews.
> 3. Don't throw it in people's faces. If people want to be preached to they'll be in church. Share with them be real. If you are real, God gets to be real through you.

I could go on and on but I won't. We'll move on down the pike. It's been a very quiet few days in the streets of Lookeba. Not seeing a lot of traffic. And other than the German Shepard and the white dog at the in town farm, we have seen no other dogs. The town dogs appear to have all the freedom. They run the town, they never have leashes, and they rummage through the garbage for extra food. They rarely leave Lookeba. Our dogs are on leashes all the time. They have to go to school, at least Dutchess does. She brings her homework home for Elizabeth Taylor because sharing is important. They will get to go to ball games, dog parks, hospitals, and they get to go to Minnesota in March. So who has more freedom? The obedience merits all sorts of other rewards. Live with their masters, getting lots of lovins, and treats that haven't been discarded or are past their expiration dates.

Melisa talked to all four of us about preaching last night. We talked about how it went. What she did well and what stood out. I asked her what, if anything, she learned. She told me that she was never going back. She'd preach wherever she could. She committed herself to it. I thought about Job being faithful and committed to God. I thought about the New Year's resolutions that seem to have no staying power. They seem to cycle back again every year or every couple of years. This is more like Jonah who spent his whole chapter fighting with God and reluctantly doing his calling and finished by complaining to God. Dutchess is going to ride my commitment to the completion of her obedience classes. Her resulting obedience will allow her greater and greater freedom. She will be able to go further and further from home. She will earn more and more trust by her master. The better she is, the

Walking With God

more treats she gets. I've always fancied my dog a role model. So let's be like Dutchess.

February 23rd
Go with the Flow

Life is all about ebb and flow. There is an "intelligent design" that goes into life. How's that for sticking a buzzword into my entry.

Here in Oklahoma, we drill for oil and natural gas. My wife was commenting on how quickly once a rig is shut down after it is started. "Don't they pump until it dries up?" she asked Mark, a veteran of the oil fields as a welder. He informed her of the vast network of underground pipe that directs oil once a well is activated. Staying on pipes and pipeline, the thing about a pipeline, when it's doing what it is designed to do, it is full, and it never stagnates. We need to be full and flowing into the lives of those around us. It's about watering seeds and letting others water your seeds. We need to be pipes filled with living water. The network of oil pipes is like our vessels. The oil flows and is directed through a series of valves. We have to learn to go with the flow. There are going to be pipes that get clogged or seals that leak, but we need to redirect our energy around the problem and not let it bring us to a screeching halt. Redirect and keep moving forward, a simple lesson from the oil wells.

About mid way through our walk, Dutchess stuck her nose to the ground and didn't lift it up for a couple of hundred feet. It was as if Scooby Doo had been bribed with a Scooby Snack to attack the bad guy, and "curse you meddling kids," was moments away. I'd never seen her track anything and I had no idea what had intrigued her nose. She is a terrier and born to hunt. It got me thinking what is tracking, and is it what you were born to do? She seemed perfectly at ease doing the bloodhound thing. I hope to have that same comfort level in my endeavors. Take some time to get to know yourself, re-examine what scents have your attention. Is it money, friends, or maybe acceptance (Matthew 6:33)?

The very first small group we did was "The Purpose Driven Life" by Rick Warren. He didn't make himself a millionaire by writing something that was just a bunch of fluff that was Danielle Steele's job. Read it. Look for your natural fit. Pray about it and follow it. You'll be happier, and your pipeline will be filled with happiness to flow into other people's lives.

February 25th
A Guest Writer

In an effort to get the coveted "Wife of the Year Award," I decided to let my wonderful husband sleep in today. You see, the past few weeks have been non-stop days filled to overflowing with every imaginable event. We spent yesterday going to two weddings only after Steven worked a half shift. The weddings were both fabulous and we certainly were blessed to have been in attendance. However, all the festivities left Steven exhausted. Anyway, I'm sure you get the picture. So I decided to take 100 pounds of Airedale walking their required 2.2 miles.

You should know however, they didn't get to walk yesterday. So as you can imagine they were very excited about the walk today. I felt a little like Jesus must have felt when the disciples were arguing over who got to sit on his right side in heaven. Just getting out the door was a trying event. Elizabeth Taylor and Dutchess have to sit and stay

Walking With God

seated until their master goes out the door in front of them. We are still working on this and believe me some days they are great and some days they are not so great. Try to get both of them to sit and keep Cash, the golden retriever, from getting out the door and you could almost decide to skip the whole walk. But alas, this girl is not a quitter. After finally getting out the door, a task that took a mere seven minutes, we head off on our merry way.

We had made it out the drive, up the hill and had started down the hill when who comes running up behind us, but our friend and past journal entry celebrity...Dixie, the walker coon dog. I'm thinking great, here we go again, Dixie is always a distraction to the dogs. So I was not so happy to see she had brought a friend, the next-door neighbor's dog (I don't know his/her name, but for the sake of this journal entry I will call her Tag Along). I'm sure the sight was funny to everyone except maybe ME! Once again abandoning the walk flashed through my brain as a viable option. Once again I remembered I was not a quitter and soon the ladies and I settled back into our normal walking pace. I noticed that about the time we passed Roger's Service Station, the next-door neighbor's dog, Tag Along, had decided that she had gone just about far enough. She gave up on the walk and just turned back.

I looked ahead and noticed that our friend, the lovable Dixie, was way ahead leading the pack once again joining us for a walk. The thought came to me that this was a wonderful example of how some people do their walk with God. They start out thinking how wonderful walking with God is and before long they tire and give up and go back to the things they know and are comfortable with. While others get excited about their walk with God and race ahead in excitement, oblivious to the fact that they have left God in the dust. While still others who have been trained by the Master remain closely at His side their entire walk.

This visual lesson is one we work to learn every day. Yes, there were times when the ladies had to be reminded to heel and remain at the side of the master and there may be times when we have to have the same reminder, but it is much easier to fall back into place when you are close enough to hear the gentle voice of the master. As I continued to think about this simple yet profound lesson, I renewed my desire to continue to work daily to keep myself close to the side of the Master.

February 26th
Bouncing Off the Walls

A little late start, but out the door we went. The ladies were like kids at Christmastime. The extra waiting got them extra antsy this morning. To them the walk is like Christmas day. They get so excited. It is such a stark contrast to how they behave the rest of the time. I'm sitting on my couch and I don't even know they are here. That's how reserved they usually are.

How many people sleepwalk through their day? They are like the little man from the Dunkin Donuts commercial getting up saying, "Gotta make the donuts." What are we getting excited about? I get excited about date nights with my wife, football games, big events like concerts and I even get excited about the prospect of doing nothing. Down time is getting so rare that it is exciting to do nothing.

The dogs tend to act like the walk is the greatest thing

in the world. They step completely out of character because it is so much better than the rest of their day. What is the greatest thing in your world? What causes you to get out of your head with excitement? The greatest thing in the world is the presence of God so why don't I seek Him out all day long? I get lazy. I get distracted and preoccupied. I think the dogs would walk 15 miles a day if we could do it without dropping dead. It's their best thing and they are smart enough to know it. We need to wise up and follow their lead. Pursue the greatest thing in the world, and you won't have wasted your efforts, and will have the greatest reward.

February 27th
Relationships…What???

The impact of the two weddings I attended Saturday seems to be lingering still. I have been so thankful for the vitality of my marriage. One couple from our small group got married they had a beautiful wedding in a beautiful setting.

Melisa and I were thanking God for our small group and we prayed that everyone in our group would become fully engaged in the conversational process. From there we jumped to the eligibility of a couple of our small group members and toyed with some prospective matchmaking. She seemed to like her idea a lot and my idea met with decidedly less enthusiasm and the advice "that I needed to pray about it." That is Christianese for "you're wrong and God isn't so check with Him."

Our story is well documented among the circle we run with. We met online at a Christian website, The

Christian Café. The same website, which later banned us because we were married (Please see my earlier entry on religion and relationship). I am from Minneapolis, a metro area of 2 million, and Melisa from Lookeba town of 800, with the nearest big town an hour away. I tried and had several disastrous online relationships. She tried and had an unsuccessful 20-year marriage. This was all to polish off the rough edges so we'd fit perfectly with one another. We aren't perfect, but we both believe we are perfect for one another. That being said we wholeheartedly endorse including God in the dating process as well as keeping Him at the center of our relationship. Dogs on the other hand go the complete opposite route. They go into heat and through hell or high water, they're gonna get themselves a little somethin' somethin'. While a great way to propagate the species, it's not a good way to enjoy a rich and satisfying relationship. Dogs aren't even comforted by the lie that "they will call you later."

So we asked God into our matchmaking. If we are going to meddle in people's lives, we want to have the heavenly stamp of approval. Part of being a "good" Christian is living out what you talk about. Anyone can talk a good game, but if it's just talk, then it doesn't get you past the sound of your own voice. I'm sure most people want to move beyond how far their voice can carry them.

We had talked for years about supporting some of

the ministries that had fed us spiritually and because we've purchased teachings from some of them have been asked to partner with them. I've always felt put off by these requests. They aren't any different than Ford or Chevy trying to convince me to put my money in what they provide. The difference, however, is scriptural (Matthew 10:41-42). There is a promise that you share in the anointing of the prophet you support. This isn't emptying our wallets to someone in hopes that he will tell God to drop a bag of money at our front door. It's about committing to support a ministry that teaches what the Bible says. The anointing that Jesus brought, freedom from burdens (Matthew 16: 16; Isaiah 10:26).

We thought about what we needed deliverance from. We aren't sick, but we're not healthy either. We thought about health and about money. We're not rich, but we are not poor either. We're exercising and we are exercising fiscal restraint, but progress seems hardly measurable. So we decided to employ some scriptural remedy to our lives instead of just talking about it. We will walk the walk and not just talk the talk. This morning we walked the dogs and talked to God. Which will enable us to do both the walking and the talking of a Christian life.

It's ugly mirror of truth time. Walking the walk and talking the talk got thrown in our face Sunday night. It wasn't even thrown. Our son Levon gently applied the truth like washing the dirt off a face of a youngster. We had all the kids over for dinner Sunday and conversation slowly turned to a critique of Mark's lifestyle. Mariah left to go to watch TV. Mark went with Levon into his room and the rest of us complained about what Mark did or didn't do for 30 minutes or so. Eventually the claws subsided. The frustration over his imperfection was vented. There was no addressing our own shortcomings (Matthew 7:3; Luke 6:41). Levon came into the room and pointed out how unkind we were and perhaps we needed to reconsider how we talked (Isaiah 11:6). He didn't blast us with judgment (Matthew 7:1). He simply pointed out in his laid back style, a way we could live a better life (Proverbs 27:17).

Bear with me. This next segue is going to be a little bumpy. I don't recall how we got on it. Oh, yes I do. We were praying about God intervening in relationships and I got to thinking about deals I'd made with God when I was dating. If He would get me a girlfriend I'd do XYZ. A coworker of mine told me of how he'd honored a deal he had made with God and forsaken Godiva Chocolates. He's a different breed of cat. He refers to himself as very, very gay. Melisa and I talked about what is the best way to show Him God's love; love him and not his lifestyle. Reach out to him to show him the value God has for him in how you treat him. Withholding judgment is so hard to do in a society that lives to divide. The Bible speaks of being in the world and not of the world, and being not conformed to the world but being transformed by the renewing of your mind (Romans 12:2).

March 2nd
A Man Alone (With Two Ladies)

Melisa, staring down the barrel of her month-end paperwork deadline, gave the walk a pass this morning. Sadly it wasn't to sleep in or relax. It was to work.

So the ladies and I headed out into the cold cruel world. We didn't know which of the many perils of early morning Lookeba we would have to face. Would it be fresh road kill, the return of Dixie, or perhaps a deer carcass strung up on the bridge; all of which we've had to deal with at one time or another.

I headed out and hot on the heels of my pondering precious metals and their purification, I asked for an impressionable heart. If your heart isn't impressionable, then nothing that is put there stays. Have you ever tried to impress something on a manhole cover or a tree stump? How was your success level?

Walking With God

Mariah and her friend, Colyn are doing a demonstration for 4H about how to make play dough. Now there is something that is impressionable. Another world-class impressionable plaything is Silly Putty. It is always the children's toys that keep their impressions the longest. Just like children's minds and children's hearts. I haven't seen a Mazzarotti or a set of golf clubs that are very impressionable. Be childish. Ditch all the preconceptions that growing up has placed in your hearts like so much arterial plaque. Clean out your system. Get rid of that which hardens and start with a fresh impressionable heart.

My father, John Zimmerman, would say, "Thirsty people want beer not explanation." This would not list with the great religious doctrines of our time, but is a wonderfully practical truth. Thirsty people want something to drink (Matthew 25:35). You don't ever get your thirst met by waiting for the Culligan Man to swing by your circumstances. Be proactive. The whine of, "But I just don't know what do to" is echoing in bedrooms, boardrooms, down high school hallways and off cubicle walls all over America (James 1:5-6; Matthew 7:8). If somebody has done what you want to do, or overcome similar obstacles you face, ask them about it. We aren't powerless and we have God who is way beyond anything our little minds can deal with. So there is always a way for your thirst to be quenched. Drink deep.

March 4th
Choosing to Heal

Melisa and I started off on the wrong foot this morning. Never a good thing when the primary activity is walking. Fortunately, the stumble was spiritual and momentary. I brought up doing the right things for the wrong reasons or doing the right thing, then gripping about it. Melisa thought I was going after her when I was going after a behavior we are both guilty of doing. Once my intentions were made clear, things settled down. We started talking about my very sad ability to keep score on everything. A stat freak growing up, I memorized baseball cards. I knew batting averages and pitchers wins and losses like some people remember birthdays and phone numbers. I was now twisting that ability into a running list of IOUs for everyone we knew. None of my wonderful good deeds were provided with the provision that a good deed is to be done to me in return. God knowing what was going on in my head had a series of sermons lined up at Victory Church on manipulation which started four hours after this mornings walk ended.

Melisa said to me, "Think about the dogs for a second. They probably would rather run off with Dixie than walk with us." I've seen how animated they get when we mix a little running with the walking. I suspect they would rather run. They heel when we ask them and don't ask for a treat or even lovins when they do. There are no scores being kept, no IOUs being written. There isn't even a dirty look shot in our direction. There is just a response to the request of their master. Our master asks us to love the Lord our God with all our heart, mind, and strength. The second request is likewise, to love each other as we love ourselves (Mark 12:30-31). He doesn't even do a backwards correction on our leashes. So let's choose to heal.

March 7th
Come Fly Away

Today is going to be short and hopefully sweet. I didn't jot down my notes and I am writing it a day later, so I've already let a good portion fall out of the ear opposite the one it entered by. This is the point that absolutely stuck with me. We've had both dogs groomed recently. And that requires their ears to be shaved. Their ears have gone from shaggy to sleek, very representative of the dog's appearance in general. We were walking along and I noted their ears bouncing up and down. I commented on how it looked like they were trying to fly, but were not very aerodynamically designed. Melisa astutely commented on how I shouldn't say that to the bumblebee.

It got us on the topic of God and the impossible (Philippians 4:13). Scientist still haven't determined how a bumblebee can fly. It is aerodynamically flawed. Only God! If God can make the bumblebee fly, what seemingly impossible circumstance can He make an impact on in your life? Sherlock Holmes was attributed the quote, "When you have eliminated the impossible, whatever remains, however impossible, must be the truth." This leads us to the second member of the animal kingdom that came into the discussion, the platypus. The platypus is the most unlikely of all animals, part bird, part amphibian, and part mammal. It's so goofy it gets picked last after the goats and donkeys at animal kickball. Just as an aside, horses and ostriches are picked first because they are great kickers and are really fast. How unlikely an animal is the platypus? It is the only egg-laying mammal, period. It is literally one in a million, and so are you! I don't claim to be so wise that I know God's purpose for the platypus. I do know, just like each of us, the platypus was created for a purpose. I do know that we do have a purpose (Romans 8:28; Romans 9:17; 2 Corinthians 5:5). In the middle of this entry we changed the radio to hear Chris Tomlin sing, "We Were Meant To Be." Einstein, a fairly respected and intelligent man said, "We are not accidents, neither are our circumstances." Seek God and you will go a long way to finding out why you're here and what you're supposed to be doing.

March 9th
Strangers in a Strange Land

I have to start off by bragging on our dogs. They made a 13-hour car trip and were great! They got to my sister's house and didn't jump all over her kids or misbehave. They made us realize how a good dog can be enrichment in your life. My six-year-old niece and five-year-old twin nephews fed and watered them. It was so cute.

We got up like we always do around 6:00am. It was quiet, the blankets were warm and the temptation to roll over and go back to sleep came and went. The dogs were kenneled up downstairs and were very happy to see us.

Out we went, not knowing where we were going or how far we'd go. We headed out through the plowed sidewalks of Apple Valley, MN. The snow was as tall as the dogs. They had seen snow and walked in it in Oklahoma, but not in this kind of volume. Dutchess didn't seem too impressed, but Elizabeth Taylor seemed to love it. She climbed right up on the bank to do what dogs do on walks. She ambled down onto the sidewalk when I first noticed the height of the bank. If the obstacle is as big as you are, you've got a choice. Surrender to it or climb on top if it and be twice as tall as you were before. On our way, I read an article in *Relevant* magazine about chasing lions. Benaniah came across a lion and rather than run from it he chased it. He and the lion wound up in a pit. Instead of going from bad to worse, Benaniah thought, "Now he can't get away in this snowy, slippery place. I'm going to kill me a lion." How many of us see our obstacles as huge snow banks towering as tall as we are, or as lions? How many of us see them as chances to come out better?

A little side note: Earlier I'd written about avoiding ruts and routines. I add this, when you leave the completely familiar places, sometimes a little touch of what you know is nice. On, our walk, we were coming back and there was a city bus coming the other way. The bus wasn't driven by Joe Rodriguez, a local school bus driver, but it just made us think that God had made a seamless transition from Oklahoma to Minnesota. He is ahead of the game and always where we are regardless of whether we take the time to talk to Him or not. So take the time to talk to Him. He loves it and you'll be richer for it. I'll write more from the great white north tomorrow. All this snow

Steven Zimmerman

is just God's way of helping me appreciate Oklahoma a little bit more.

March 10th
Miles and Mick

Back in the old neighborhood and the ladies seemed a little bit spoiled by their trips to the dog park in Minnesota. They were a little bit "pully" today. I tried to put a positive spin on it. They aren't disobedient. They are trying to give our arms a better workout. We started out our walk thanking God for the blessed life we lead. Having spent the weekend with my family and my friends from Minnesota, I got caught up to a certain extent with their lives. I am in the middle of a struggle with comparison. This, however, came in handy when everyone else's big problems seemed bigger than mine and their smaller problems seemed more numerous than mine. This is not a proclamation of my perfection, but the foundation for our gratitude. We are blessed, fortunate and to be envied.

This morning we started out celebrating where we are and looking forward to where we are going. The reason we went to Minnesota was for the memorial dinner for my dad. He's now been dead as long as he and my mom had been married. The tradition is a spaghetti dinner and afterward, we go around the table and each give our high and low for the year. This was particularly emotional this year. There were many tears shed. I shed mine during my high; others shed tears of pain during their lows. I told Melisa on our walk this morning there is no reason we can't reach out to those family members who are hurting. I drive 70 miles to work every day. I told her armed with my cell phone I am going to reach out to those whose tears of pain I watched fall. I likened it to the traveling medicine show. The difference is I don't stop, and I try to sell love and support not snake oils and fake medicine. It doesn't cost me anything. It won't make me late for anything, and it is a chance to sow into some people's lives.

  The astute reader has already made a mental note, "Hey what does this have to do with the miles and Mick? He hasn't even mentioned the dogs outside the opening paragraph." How right you are faithful and intelligent reader. Please check the appropriate space, more flattery ____ less flattery ____.

  We started talking about the difference having God with us versus not having God made in our happiness. Without God, you get as far as you can take yourself. The quarters were inserted and the mental pinball was released in my brain. I went from being part of a group with God and fellow believers to pray for you and encourage you to being a solo act. Miles Davis is a brilliant soloist. I compared him to Joe Williams, the brilliant jazz vocalist, whose fame was gained while singing with a band, be it Count Basie or some other leader. The ball hit the cushion and ricocheted to Mick Jagger. He is one of the most famous front men in the history of rock-n-roll. Million selling albums, sold out concerts are a foregone conclusion. You never see a Rolling Stones album in the discount rack. Now, to the challenge: name for me one of Mick Jagger's greatest hits as a solo artist? Can you even tell me the names of his three albums? I am willing to claim to now have the only devotional book that makes this statement, "Be like Mick Jagger." Get hooked up with the right band mates and carve out your space in history!

    I find myself healthy and happy by hooking up with God. I'd recommend it to everyone. Melisa's passion is not music so she added this, "How does this relate to the dogs?" I had no idea. Dogs are happier and more balanced when they are a member of a pack. The pack leader makes the rules and keeps the pack members in line. A new dog that joins the pack is surrounded by dogs whose behavior is in accordance with the pack rules. Are you a part of a pack? Whose pack are you a part of? Take a look at yourself. Put yourself in a position to have your joy, peace, and happiness increased. Find the right pack and join the right band. Enrich yourself. It will allow you to reach out and enrich others.

March 17th
Dead Skunk on the Side of the Road

The easy way out is to do a St. Patrick's theme (Matthew 7:13-14). Easy isn't always the best. Besides who can pass up a good London Wainwright III reference? There are a couple of entries that are going to be entered in reverse order because I want to get this down when it is fresh.

Melisa had been away at a baseball tournament/festival. A festival is just Oklahoma's way of saying we want to charge admission, but we don't want to have to buy a trophy. This lead to a walk that was heavy on talk and short on prayer. The rambunctious Cash joined us. Not just Cash, Cash unleashed. Cash was infusing the dogs with more energy than they needed. Then just before the bridge he bolts, throws himself down on the ground and starts flopping around like a fish on a dock. My first thought was "Oh great road kill." It gets worse. What is the last animal you want your pet to roll around with?

Your choices are:

1. A skunk
2. A skunk
3. A dead skunk

If you chose three you would be correct. It's bad enough that Levon's gentle giant was misbehaving, but then he ducked under a fence and started to chase some cows. Out here in the country, that'll get a dog shot. In a cattle farmer's eyes a stray dog is not worth one cow or calf that might get hurt during the chase. To keep our son's dog alive we got him and leashed him. I hope I wasn't rewarding him for bad behavior. We took the rest of the walk with an air of tension waiting for the next bad behavior. Tension, according to the Dog Whisperer, is a classic recipe for bad behavior. But, we saw none. We were almost back home as we got to the pungent road kill and I asked, "What would make Cash want to roll around with a dead skunk?" Melisa's response was, "What would make us want to roll around in sin?" (Romans 7:15-20). Just like that, God made His presence known. He was hanging out without saying much and when we were done with catching up, He let us know He had something for us today. Today and every day God is there for us. We just have to ask what He has to say.

March 16th
A Man Alone

There is always the temptation to sleep in when Melisa isn't home, whether she is staying in the hospital with her Dad or in this case when she is in Preston, Oklahoma with Levon's baseball team. One of the great things about getting a dog for each of us is even when she is home, is when one of us wants to sleep the other will be brave and get out from under the covers and encourage the other to get up and get dressed. The dogs operate in a pack. Dutchess and Elizabeth Taylor were a pack unto themselves as the outdoor dogs at their old house. The indoor dogs came out every now and then, but never really bonded. We brought them here and socialized them with Cash and Gerty and they have a new pack and a new pack leader.

Cash, who is pack leader, came from the pound. He didn't have a pack to lean on or be friends with. The ladies and I reminded me of the difference between being like

Cash or single guys and being part of a team like I am with Melisa.

When we get home from the walk one of us feeds the dogs and one of us makes the coffee. Come 7:30am, one of us gets Mariah up and one of us gets Levon up. The two of us make short work of the morning chores. Burdensome, but it sure is much easier with a second person (Genesis 2:22-23; Ecclesiastes 4:8-9).

We aren't to the point where we let the ladies run off leach. One thing sticks in my mind. If one got loose, she would come back. Why? Life without her sister is unfathomable. That's how it's gotten with Melisa. I can't imagine what life would be like without her. The drop off in quality is evident even in walking and caring for the dogs for one morning. There is something to being part of a pack of two. You don't have to be married to be "packed up." You can be a Ted Kaczynski, living in a hut in Montana, all alone and still hook up and let God be your pack leader. There is never any reason to be alone if you don't choose to. There are plenty of reasons to "pack up," scripturally and otherwise. So what are you waiting for?

March 28th
I Don't Need to See Clearly Now

We did our walk today and Mariah came with. She has decided to do the Oklahoma City Bombing Memorial Children's Marathon. She announced afterward she wouldn't be going with us on any more walks because she "was tired all day." If you put a clothing store, a toy store and a Wal-Mart every quarter of a mile, I can see her hopping right back on the training bandwagon.

Mariah is now sporting new glasses. For Mariah, it is not so much a vision correction as it is a chance to accessorize. During the walk she commented on how dark it was. Halfway through our walk, the road we take out of town runs out of streetlights. We told her she needed to be bold about sharing Jesus. She might be someone's last streetlight and the rest of their walk would be only lit by starlight. It sounds romantic, but it's really hard to read by (Matthew 5:14-16; James 12:35-36). Those of us living a faith-based life don't need to see a light (John 8:12) to know it's there. The saying, "There's a light at the end of the tunnel" shows how tightly bound light is to hope.

Mariah's soreness was indicative of her being a new walker. Growing pains as you begin the training process. It is just like when you begin your walk with God. There are growing pains; spiritual shin splits if you will. Mine especially is pride. My ideas were so right, so sound, I didn't need to back down from any of them. If there was a wrong done to me, I didn't have any obligation to forgive that wrong, not until I'd gotten an apology. I not only needed an apology, it better be a sincere one by golly or you went directly to jail, do not pass go, do not collect $200. This was the poison in the well that polluted the relationship with my brother for years. It was bringing my pride issue into the light that weakened it to the point where I had more victories than losses. That allowed me the breakthrough this February. As I write this, the same hand that holds my pen (yes I still use a pen and paper, not a computer) sports a ring that symbolizes my relationship with my brother (Matthew 7:3-6).

Put yourselves under a microscope. Don't be afraid to make sure there is plenty of light so you can see what the magnification shows you. Now you get to choose to stay the same or deal and make the changes and maybe you'll be rewarded the same way I was.

March 30th
Shut Up!!

A reoccurring theme has been living in the favor of God. We call it living in the bubble. When we were up in Minnesota, we got our nephews some bubbles and different wands to make different shaped bubbles. When you blow bubbles you can see through the bubble. We live in a bubble that allows us to see everything around us. We can interact just like the bubbles we blew with RJ and Griffin on their deck. A single act of disobedience can pop the bubble of favor (1 John 5:18; Romans 8:23). We were particularly thankful today because a tornado had missed my office by about a mile and a half. I thought about losing my life, my job, my car, and the lives of my coworkers and just said a great big thank you to God for keeping me in the bubble.

The dogs were a wee bit spastic this morning and they were very vocal about their desire to go for a walk.

We don't reward bad behavior. They stay in their kennels until they quiet down. They get rowdy, they don't get their leashes. They are smart enough to know, no leash, no walk. They need to be calm, submissive, that includes shutting their yaps so they can get out and get the walk, which is their favorite thing.

God wants to give us what we want (Matthew 7:9-11; Luke 11:13). Sometimes, we need to shut up. If you have every tried to talk to someone while they are talking to you, you get jibble-jabble. You and the person you are talking to, don't receive what the other is offering. God doesn't interrupt. So, if you don't close your mouth, He'll never speak over you and you will miss out.

What our mouths are doing is often doing nothing more than getting us in trouble anyway (gossip, 2 Corinthians; 12:20, slander Proverbs 10:18; idle chatter Job 11:3; Isaiah 58:13; Colossians 2:18) play too big a role in our daily conversations. I am not picking up a rock to throw at my readers because I am a recovering motor mouth. What is the carrot on the stick we are after? What is the desire of your heart (Psalm 21:2)? If you will be quiet, turn your ear to God and let Him, He'll tell you how to get it. Once you get it, don't be surprised if doors open and He allows you to take a great big bite of the carrot.

We started talking about the world seeing who Christ was in us better. You look at an apple tree; you see apples and know what kind of tree it is. What if there are no apples? I don't know enough about trees to identify them without their fruit. Melisa is preaching about the fruits of the Spirit on Wednesday nights at Bud Cox's church (Galatians 5:22). We are supposed to bear spiritual fruit. We have a fruit bowl that we keep on our dining room table. People see it right after they come into our house. What fruit is in your bowl? How sad it would be to have an empty fruit bowl as your centerpiece. What about a fruit bowl that only has oranges? That doesn't really make someone hungry for fruit unless they really like oranges. A variety of fruit looks better, eats better and is more likely to cause people to want what is in front of them. What are you putting in front of the people you come across? Hopefully it's something they can sink their teeth into.

March 31st
Open Arms Lifted High

We headed out, right on time after a rain out yesterday. We swing wide to avoid the lake that is now where the center of our driveway used to be. We headed out just randomly praying for people. The dogs are usually a bit edgy after a missed day, but they were on their best behavior today. We just assumed an attitude of gratefulness for a good weather day, for well-behaved dogs, for not getting hit by the tornado. We just threw our hands up and said thanks to God. We took a bit of a different path today. We went past our usual halfway point and up and down several small hills. We came to the next hill. It was a little bigger and a lot steeper. There was a telephone pole about a third of the way down. I jealously eyed that pole hoping we'd turn there. It was not to be. We kept going to the bottom of the hill. It presented the immediate obstacle of going back up the hill. This is not the last hill we climbed.

The final hill is the hill that leads up from Main Street. Sometimes the ladies pulling on their leashes gives us the extra energy we need to make it up the final hill. I got to thinking about how a big hill at the end causes you to realize sometimes you need a little help. The bigger the hill, the easier it is to realize the accomplishment of climbing it and the greater the victory. The most important victory in the history of man is the one Jesus completed the last day of his life by walking up a hill called Calvary. Jesus didn't have my over eager Airedales to help him up the hill. He did have a lonely guy drafted by the Romans. We didn't have to do any of the dying, though the best part is He did it for us.

April 7th
Levon, Cal Ripkin, and God

We had gotten past some bad, cold, and windy weather to get the dogs out. It wasn't colder than January. It wasn't significantly more windy either. We had just been looking for an excuse to stay in. My wife had just preached a sermon on faithfulness this past Wednesday. It really convicted us about being consistent about the dogs. We were once dauntless and now we doubt our consistency.

The subject for today started as so many does with God. The picture of consistency (Acts 31:6; Joshua 1:5; Hebrews 13:5) with the claim being found in Hebrews 13:8, spoke to us today. If He treated us the way we'd treated our dogs there would be a lot less people calling themselves Christians. It's certainly not the dog's fault. They display some wonderful consistency patterns. They get up at the same time. They get hyper before the walk every time. They settle down after breakfast. They are excellent role models for consistency. I guess when one of your first commands is to stay it gets drummed into you.

We started talking about baseball. Levon is a pitcher with great talent and a suspect work ethic. The result is a no hitter one day and getting pulled after the second inning the next. This frustrates his coach, him, and us. This led me to bring up Lou Gehrig whose 2,130 consecutive games was a record no one thought would be broken until Cal Ripkin Jr., played over 2,200 games in a row. Every year he hit between 250 and 318, had 20 home runs 10 years in a row, had over 20 doubles every year, and was an All-Star in two positions. He sacrificed his shortstop position by realizing his mobility was affected by his age. He stepped aside for a younger player and learned a new position that he mastered. We need to realize sometimes sacrifices are necessary to remain consistent and faithful. If you want the benefits that being counted on, trusted, and recognized, consider it might be harder than just rolling out of bed.

One of the role models I listed is the Creator of the universe, and if that's hard to get your brain around, the other is in the baseball hall of fame on the first ballot. Oh yeah, I also mentioned two of the best domestic companions on four legs, but you're probably tired of hearing about them.

April 8th
Carpentry

It's Easter. On Wednesday, Bud Cox talked about his "Un-Easter" message. Everybody knows the story of Easter so he went a different direction. I did the same thing. I went backwards. The thing I thought about this morning was Jesus the Carpenter. What does a carpenter do? He shapes wood. He crafts. He assembles and builds. That is what God does with us. The wood doesn't have a choice. We do.

Melisa told me about her first father in law, J. D. Lumpkin. He used to redo furniture. She said he'd take apart the chair entirely until it looked like kindling. He'd then refinish it and put it back together again, stronger than it was before. The hard part about letting ourselves be taken apart is that you see all your broken parts. It's ugly. It's painful. If you don't get your broken parts fixed, when somebody sits on your chair, it breaks and they could get hurt because you couldn't deal with your broken parts. Let me go back to the rebuilt chair, it gets to hold more weight. It is the chair that gets used more. It doesn't get stuck in the closet like the folding chair.

Melisa had this image of God the Father having her on His lap. I thought about the type of chair in God's den. The chair is a large wing back chair with lots of padding. Heavy, sturdy, it gives comfort and lets you feel safe. We wanted to be molded, shaped, and reassembled into that chair. Rebuilt to be the chair that God chooses to use. No hidden, broken parts-rebuilt better than before. I hear the intro to the six million dollar man. You know what? Oscar Goldman rebuilt Colonel Steve Austin. We need to let God rebuild us. We'll be worth more than six million dollars. We will be priceless.

April 10th
Childbirth by Proxy

The drum continued to beat consistency, consistency, consistency. It's not just in actions, walking the dogs, reading our Bibles, but it's an attitude, being grateful, reaching out to others, and loving everyone. We talked about a re-commitment to consistency. It's funny. I'm writing this several days after the fact sitting in our friend's, the Delk's, living room. We're staying with them to attend a baseball tournament four and a half hours away. We came Thursday and today is Saturday. The dogs haven't been walked in a few days and the rains have kept them from playing outside in their pen. It hasn't been the model of consistency we've talked about, but sometimes you need to put people, in this case Levon, not to mention Melisa and myself, ahead of the dogs. It is an encouragement to me that I'm looking forward to walking them tomorrow.

The drawback to working off notes like today is I

don't remember how we got transitioned to pushing through our problems to get on the other side. It's always darkest before the dawn. That's why a perfect God gave us a perfect example, placing Melisa, our dogs, and myself in the very darkness that the old saying talks about. We often start our walk in the darkness and finish it in the light of the dawn and nothing that's started gets finished without a little push. This is so clear to us, because every day we end our walk going up a pretty big hill. You really feel the victory when you get to the top and the house comes in to sight. I think God used darkness save the occasional streetlight or house light to keep us focused on Him.

We started talking about childbirth. It is the ultimate example of pushing through the pain and receiving the most joy inspiring, God affirming, life-changing event in your life. My mom, who is not the proper Catholic, said that the birth of a child is still in her eyes the most convincing proof of the existence of God.

The delicious irony of this conversation is the discussion of the childbirth process as an analogy of overcoming pain/obstacles to get to the amazing joy God is waiting to give to me, the stepparent who has never fathered anyone. I never felt labor pains or have known a contraction. The desire to give up is so strong when times get tough often we forget to push. My extensive Lamaze training teaches the importance of breathing and remembering to push. There is no delivery without the push. A few letters only separate the words delivery and the deliverance. They are only separated by a few pushes. What awesome thing is God working to birth in your life? Are you pushing to deliver it or are you living in the contractions? Push through it. The rainbow is the sign of hope after the storm. The child is the unlimited future after the pregnancy. Every child is birthed by the mother and has a father. Remember, as we are in the middle of pushing through our crisis, what is going to be on the other side. If we are the birth mother, we have a heavenly Father. So, embrace the push as God embraces you.

Lastly, we examined the pace of our walking. It's always a bit of a pressure to get home so I can get to work on time. We lengthened our distance in March, but if we flat line our time, it would cease to help us. What we noticed was when we have a really good talk with God, we walk faster, don't get as tired, and we don't have pain. I documented about how my wife and I help each other with the walk and how the dogs have each other. They always have had each other. The biggest help is when we acknowledge and welcome God's presence on our walk. I thought about the three-legged race from grade school. You never went as fast as running by yourself. This may be the only instance when three is not faster than two.

April 11th
Feast or Famine

This entry is not about my dating history before meeting and marrying my lovely bride. Sometimes our topic on the walk isn't dictated by what we hear on the walk, but something we hear before the walk, as was the case today. This morning on the Today show, there was a couple that had lost 300 pounds between them. This is a tender area with Melisa because she has struggled with her weight and hasn't seen progress from walking like she'd like. We headed out on an emotionally charged note. We talked about how we had to stack little victories like giving up pop, sadly limiting ourselves to one cup of coffee, and walking our dogs a lot more regularly than I've been writing. There are plenty of gems I've left on Main Street, Lookeba because I didn't write down my cliff notes after my walk.

So we talked about the white tornado approach she

takes to her work and how that approach nets immediate results and how it doesn't work with dieting. She had dropped some significant weight prior to meeting me, so we know it's doable. We decided to target water consumption. I, the guy whose idea of breakfast was hostess Ho-Ho's and Mt. Dew, is not going to claim to be either a medical or diet expert. I have, however, seen a lot of them on TV and they are unanimous in the idea that water is good for you and you need to drink lots of it. I set my sights at two liters a day. I'm not sure what Melisa's water goal is. The battleground has been set, the war continues and we are marching into it together. We expect to come out of this with another battle won in a larger war. For her it is a war with casualties and suffering. We are going to keep moving forward, keep drinking our water, and when this one is in the win column we will find our next fight to pick. Eventually the momentum will shift, and winning will get easier and more frequent. Victory will be Melisa's and I'll be more than happy to fork over my bonus check for her to get some new clothes. I am going to grab myself another 16oz bottle of Aquafina. Bottoms up!

April ??
The Lost Episode

I found some old cliff notes from a walk a while back. They're undated so we'll see how well my rapidly aging memory holds up.

We'd seen a video at Victory Church about seeing people's pain and humanity instead of just seeing them as strangers. We don't know what's going on with them. We can, however, reach out to them. The video talked about putting on "glasses of grace," seeing the neighborhood skateboarder not as a menace, but as someone who might need someone to give him some affirmation. Take a chance and see if you can meet a need, touch a life, and look a little bit more like Christ.

Meanwhile closer to home, Bud Cox had given a post Melisa sermonette (which is a term for when Bud preaches a little sermon after Melisa preaches an entire sermon) about having God's heart. It's a Bud transplant, from thug life to God's love. If you have God's heart, there aren't groups to cause division. There are only sheep in the flock. Everyone is valuable and every person deserves the best we can give him or her (Matthew 25:40). Pastor Paula, Bud's wife, was trying to teach the church the difference between blabbing to God and not letting Him get a word in edgewise and taking time to stop and hear what He was saying back to you. We all have someone in our lives who, instead of listening, spends their time planning their response while you're talking. God is NEVER like that. We need to train ourselves to hear from God.

Our dogs are being trained to hear our voice and obey our commands. The great thing about dogs, unlike people, is you never have to worry about them hearing you or talking back. You may be ignored, but you will be heard. I've heard a couple of people who have rabbit ears when other people are talking about them. We need to have spiritual dog-ears when God is talking to us.

This was a particularly busy walk. I wouldn't say I'm just getting started, but I still have plenty more from the "lost episode." The always-popular cliff notes say next on the agenda is checkbook. This always a hit or miss proposition in our house. Sometimes it's "Whoo-hoo, we've got money" and other times it is a house call from "Debbie Downer." Either way, it's a chance to exalt God over every circumstance. When I save up debit card receipts and

ATM receipts and dump them in Melisa's lap, it's a chance to trust God to either do a miracle in our finances or teach me a lesson that will prevent me from doing this in the future. The Israelites walked around the desert for 40 years. It may take a few lessons to get this down, but I suspect I'll clock in well ahead of the Israelites.

My last thought centers around a sermon preached by Bill Wilson on Isaiah 6:1-10. It's in three parts: Look up - see God for who He is and exalt Him. Look in - see who you are, what your needs and imperfections are. Look out - see others with God's heart and meet their needs and watch as God sees to it that your needs are met. Allow God to be God. Let him do the heavy lifting (Matthew 11:30). It's up to us. Ask my dogs which is easier, teaching a dog or learning to obey. I never saw Dutchess a single time lose patience or get mad at me during our time at K-9 University. Let's allow God to do the work and we can soak it up. He loves us more than enough to cover the times we don't hear and obey. Eventually we will get it right.

April 23rd
Disney Theology

Walt Disney was a different breed of cat. He, by all accounts, was a terrible boss and there aren't a lot of accounts of his great acts of kindness. He also gets to fall into that rare category of genius. I've seen TV programs that tout the genius of Disney. When you are a genius, a door of special knowledge is open to you. The reason I mention Disney is he is creator of two of the ultimate dog movies, Lady and the Tramp and the focus of my attention this morning, 101 Dalmatians.

The scene I want to focus on is when Pongo is looking out the window watching the dogs and their owners. The theory is that the dogs become like their owners and visa versa. This couldn't be truer than with Levon and his dog Cash. They are both laid back, taking life easy, spending the whole day looking for the next creek to swim in. The newest pack member, replacing the relocated

Walking With God

Gertrude D. Rockefeller, is Riley Biggens, a miniature Schnauzer puppy. He belongs to Mariah. He proves you don't have to be the same gender to transfer characteristics between dog and owner. Riley is smart. He is way further ahead of the housebreaking curve than was his predecessor. Oh, and he is high maintenance. He is very vocal. Sometimes in my head I hear Riley reciting his shopping list. Mariah and her dog are just starting the bonding process, but I see it taking root.

This is also true of husbands and wives. Prior to my moving to Oklahoma and getting married, I liked to sleep in. If I could make it to 10:30am I was thrilled. My wife was up and at 'em by 5 or 5:30am. We got married and now we meet in the middle, not perfect middle, closer to her end, but still technically in the middle. We have adopted each other's language. Before I met Melisa, I could count the times I said, "Cool beans" on my tusks. Now I say it pretty often. Melisa never said, "Dude." Now she occasionally addresses Levon as "dude." Our language, our sleep, our diets, (I now eat and enjoy broccoli), the fact that I drink more water and after years of training abstain from hot dogs, is part of our growing together. In Genesis 2:24, it describes how a man and wife will cleave to one another, as the two become one flesh. The oneness is the ideal in the physical, mental and spiritual realms. The whole idea from Jerry McGuire of "You complete me," however cheesy, is taking two unique individuals putting them together to make them more than the sum of the parts.

Finally, God made us in His image (Genesis 1:26-27: Romans 8:25). The big picture was for us to be made in His image. The $128,000 question is are we going to choose to live like Him? Are we going to take the likeness to the next level? The scriptures about being like Christ are too abundant to list. It's that whole free will thing that jumps up and bites us like the German Shepherd did Melisa when she was seven. That dog had a heart to heart with her Dad and never bit anything else again. Our free will allows us to emulate Jesus and in doing so, we become closer to being "one" with Him as much as our humanness allows. It is about completion not perfection. We need to adopt a James 4:8 attitude. If we desire to draw near to God by choosing to act like Him, He will draw near to us. Couple that with Jeremiah 29:13, a Scripture co-opted by popular culture "seek and you will find." It's how we head into our walk. Melisa says she sees God sitting on our front step waiting for us. We head out looking for Him and expecting Him to show up, which leads to Isaiah 30:18 (you are going to need an Amplified Bible to get the full impact) and you've got the ideal equation. God designed our relationship and our gradual transformation into a closer representative of Christ.

Walking With God

So go back and rent 101 Dalmatians and think about God and you when the scene play. If you don't want to that's okay, get it for the song, "Cruella DeVille" a top 10 Disney villain. Then find the cover of it by The Replacements both are worth your time. Too much to do for this day, so I'll wrap up.

April 24th
Armed and Dangerous

We had the seed for this morning's topic planted last night. We were watching Joel Osteen preach and he talked about making the devil wish you'd stayed in bed. You want him to say, "Oh dang, they're up again." It all starts with how we see ourselves. It works best when we see ourselves as God sees us (Philippians 4:13; Romans 8:17; Romans 8:37; 2 Timothy 2:3).

We are called to be many things and God never runs us down. One of the things we need to know is we are called to be soldiers for Christ. As parents of a soldier, we prefer spiritual warfare to anything going on in Iraq. Soldiers always have a battle plan. Here's the not so random book plug, "The Purpose Driven Life" by Rick Warren helps you get that plan. Reading your Bible helps you get the battle plan.

My wife is a planner. She has plans A-F in place

and is working on plan G in case the first six don't work out. She wants me to have a five-step action plan for taking out the trash. I usually break out in a rash if there is too much planning involved. I wear out the seat of my pants like some people wear out socks. Apparently since the Wright Brothers did their thing there are better things to fly by than the seat of your pants. Who knew?

A soldier needs the right equipment. I see on the news the tug of war over the funding bill for the Iraq war and whether or not there is a pull out time attached. No politician wants to be the one who takes the gun out of the hands of the soldiers and the bullets out of their guns. Just like them, we aren't going to win without the supplies we need to be victorious. There is only one offensive weapon in the armor of God, the Word (Ephesians 6:10-17). There is also no protection for your back. There is no retreat.

So suit up, grab your gear, and get your battle plans. The difference is this battle is already won, while human conflict is undecided. We will need to make a decision so let's pick our fights wisely. Let's go out and get the victory.

May 9th
On Hold

We were starting to feel a little bit like the Cleveland Indians, who started out their home season with four consecutive snowed out games. The rain left us temporarily and we squeezed in a quick 1.6 miles. The ladies had to wait for several days for the walk they to enjoy. They waited for the most part with a good attitude. They were finally rewarded with what they wanted. The rain, a situation beyond our control, took away their walks but didn't sour their mood. Patience was eventually rewarded.

There have been some unexpected events that have come up which have left us scratching our heads. Our long term plan, our vision, has always involved moving to Oklahoma City, going to Bible school at Victory Church, hooking up with the a Victory Church plant, serving in the ministry, and starting the Bridge Builder Retreat Center.

Melisa has recently been given the opportunity to

preach in Hinton, which she seized and embraced the opportunity. There is a bond that has been forged with the pastor in Hinton. When we asked Bud what the next step was, he said we just needed to get the word out, letting people know she was preaching which would get her invitations to churches. Bud said he would put in a good word for her.

Melisa, being the go-getter she is, set up an appointment with the woman who married us. She is the pastor of the Elk City Community Church about an hour west. Judy, the pastor, mentioned how nice it would be to take a vacation and how welcome Melisa and I would be. I've always liked Elk City.

Shortly after this meeting, we got to the finals of the state baseball tournament and another weird, out of left field event happened. Levon gets hit in the face by a pitch and we spend most of the day in the hospital. I'm still not sure how that fit into the equation, but it does. He is doing better than can be expected. What we were expecting to cause major dental work will not. Thank you, God. He has the surgery to get the rest of the solution in place on Friday. While we were in the waiting room, Shirley Votaw, one of our best friends from Victory Church told me that she was going to be moving. This was a shock to me. She and her husband are our role models at Victory. When you find out your going to lose an anchor, sometimes you start tossing to and fro before it's actually gone.

All these things added together made us wonder if the original plan was still in play. What are we supposed to do? Stay the course? Move to Elk City? Stay here and invest our time in Hinton? As captain of the ship that is my family this is a decision I want to get right. No one wants to move his family out of the will of God. Until Levon's health took over the top spot, I've been praying about this decision like none other. As we were walking today, I got my answer...wait! I had waiting on my mind when I got home. Normally I'd have been really ticked off by that answer, "What do you mean wait? I want an Oompa Loompa and I want it now." Today I looked up wait in my concordance when I got back, a little sweaty, but none the worse for wear. Here's what I found out. Nothing bad ever happened to anyone who waited.

Psalm 27:14: Waiting produced a stout heart.
Psalm 130:5: Waiting produced hope.
Acts 1:4: The result of waiting was the arrival of the gifts of the Holy Spirit.

It goes on like that everywhere wait is used. So I'll wait and serve while I'm waiting because God doesn't throw changeups. He will honor my waiting and my obedience with something so awesome it can only come from Him.

May 4th
What's in a Name?

We've recently added a temporary member to our pack. A yellow lab we've dubbed Slick. Slick sits, fetches and clearly was someone's pet. He certainly wasn't called Slick because he ignores us when we call him that. Slick puts us over the 200-pound dog limit and is in gross violation of the no shed policy Melisa has in place. Cash, the golden retriever mix was grandfathered in on that one. The ladies went through a transition period when we first got them, changing their names.

    My sister, out of nowhere, decided I needed a nickname and decided I should be called Beeperjoe. I thought it was ridiculous and baseless. It proved to be both, but it stuck like glue anyway. I hated it for a while, but it eventually became uncle Beeper. Instead of shuddering at it I now answer to it. People often grow into their names.

Butch rarely grows up to be a concert pianist. There aren't a lot of cage fighters named Melvin. We were trying to come up with a name for our non-profit organization. We weren't very successful. We kept at it though and thought we had one, "Yesterday's Cocoon Ministries," but everyone we talked to said they had no idea what it meant. So we will go back to the drawing board. There are over 100 names for God in the Bible. He "has grown" into all of them. Are we growing into our names? Father, husband, and friend, all leave a little room for improvement in our lives. What choices are we making that are helping us grow into our names?

Melisa was just fooling around on the internet and stumbled across a nine bedroom, eight bath, 7,000 square foot bed and breakfast/conference center for sale in Sulphur, Oklahoma. We were both excited. It has previously been used as a retreat center for pastors and a ministry headquarters, which was exactly what we were looking for. We found this amazing property. The only flaw was we wanted it on a lake. This is near a lake, but not on it. The other major stumbling block was we lacked the $400,000 to purchase it and we have no experience running a bed and breakfast or a conference center.

We are both absolutely willing to learn and try because we know we will ultimately be in the service of pastors and have a retreat center for the restoration of relationships. The question was what to do with the discovery of this place. My wife, the white tornado, had envisioned having her road trip to Sulphur to take the owners out to dinner, immediately opening up negotiations. My approach was a little different. I suggested we pray and wait to hear from God. She thought my plan lacked being proactive. I thought it had the least chance for no wasted effort. Efficiency is activity I tried to explain. I wasn't proposing sitting on our backsides waiting for God to put the next step in green paint across the sky. I just wanted to do what God wanted us to do. There were things that in the interim had to be done regardless. Like get our non-profit filed and created. Get through graduation season. We didn't figure out what was next, but we did decide whatever it was we were going to be in agreement on it (Philippians 1:27; James 1:8; Matthew 18:19). So once we find that accord we will move forward. Until then, a little heated fellowship never hurt anyone.

May 21ST
All Good and Perfect Gifts

Let's get this out of the way first off; Melisa and I are fine, the dogs are fine. It was a little like the Wizard of Oz and we got swept up in a vortex of laziness. There was some rain early on, but as of late it has been worshipping at the St. Mattress Cathedral. It is really sad, considering the state of our mattress that we would choose that over endorphin releasing exercise and spirit lifting time with God. My decision to break the cycle of laziness started yesterday. We returned again to our wonderful morning walk with dogs. God was everywhere all day long. We had at power outage a church, but it didn't affect our classroom except that it took out the TV. This allowed for us to just talk which was really cool.

From there we had our small group expo. We got free shirts and had our best ever responses from people asking about the small group program. Did I mention free

Walking With God

Buffalo Wild Wings and Marble Slab ice cream? That was followed by a great sermon on the five love languages; a central pillar Melisa and I view on how to build a healthy relationship.

The big surprise came after church when friends of ours gave us their Suburban. I had never been given a car before as an adult. I'd been lent money for one, (thanks, Mom) but never given a car. That was followed by lunch at Buffalo Wild Wings, (which is owned and operated by a member of our church) which was excellent and the company of the Yost's and Rick Ramsey was even better than the food.

We got home and got treated with friendly receptive kids who were eager to spend time with us, especially Mariah, who even asked us to wake her up so she could have coffee with us in the morning (no she doesn't drink coffee she drinks green tea). The reason I rehashed all this is it's easy to recognize gifts when they are obvious. We got outside today with the dogs and it was perfect, sunny, 73 degrees, without wind. We couldn't have had a better day if we'd designed it. There are gifts big and small we are given every day (James 1:16). The question is how many gifts fly under the radar? I'm grateful that Melisa and I recognize our triumphant return to dog walking was greeted with a fabulous day. My mother advocates the idea of saving up all the little delights so you have then to enjoy when the big disaster hits. This is along those lines. I think we need to say thank you as we collect our little treasures. T. Harv Ecker says, "Whatever you focus on grows." By taking the time to stop and say thanks, we spend a little focus on the good things that show up. The more focus the easier it is to see. We can multiply the good things, big and little, by getting better at seeing them and focusing on them when they show up.

It brought to mind how easy it is to become spoiled, ungrateful little kids. I grew up Catholic so I had godparents. Mine are Jim and Sherry Flanery, long time friends of my parents. I am the only kid in my family that doesn't have aunts and uncles as godparents. I was eight or nine and we were celebrating Christmas at my Grandma Pierre's house. We all got a present from Grandma and Grandpa. My bother and two sisters got presents from their godparents. I had my one present and I was done. Eight year olds don't respond well to sitting and watching other people open presents. I let my parents know how unhappy I was. Then my mom let me know how unhappy she was. She had authority behind her position. I just had whininess. What I missed was my healthy family; a gift that ten years later, wouldn't include my dad or my Grandpa Pierre. I missed it as an eight year old, but see it now 32 years later. I implore you, look around. See little gifts. Christmas, birthdays, Suburban's; those are easy.

Walking With God

Let's see the hard to see gifts. They are like Waldo. They are there, just a little harder to see. Keep looking!

We were headed up the hill on our way home and across the road wandered a cat. Dutchess and Elizabeth Taylor thought this was God's gift to them. I am very thankful Dutchess didn't pull my arm out of it's socket. It was a low point for my obedience school graduate, but in the end, I outweigh her by 135 pounds and despite having surprise on her side, I won. Melisa commented on it being their flesh. Dogs have instincts and don't usually override them like people do. Romans 7:5 is one of many Scriptures that warn us against listening to our bodies and going off chasing cats. The common misconception is that there is an all out ban on fun if you don't chase cats. Outside of narcotics, I chased my share of cats and they are nothing more than a sugar spike. How does fullness of joy sound (Psalm 16:11)? Or peace that passes all understanding (Philippians 4:7)? A little submission goes a long way. A little God covers a lot of ground and there isn't a hangover the next morning. Save your aspirin for when you hit your thumb with a hammer or something drops on your foot. Avoid chasing your flesh and enjoy the great gifts God has for us each day. The tradeoff is more than you can think, hope or imagine.

May 25th
Her Mouth Runneth Over

We were barely out the door when Melisa started talking. It was to be the theme for the day. My job was to listen, trying to retain as many nuggets as she could spit out. It is probably easier to come up with material when the burden of being brilliant (insert tongue in cheek) is lifted. The value of listening, however, cannot be overlooked. The old line about two ears and one mouth comes to mind. There are a bundle of verses about the mouth and the ears (Proverbs 10:19; Proverbs 21:23; James 1:26).

    The ladies bounded out of their cages with the usual vigor. Surely as the sun rises in the east and sets in the west, the Airedales will be spazzes if they think there is a walk involved. I'm even afraid of writing it instead of spelling it out to avoid sending them into a frenzy.

    Out of the box, Melisa says we need to have the same enthusiasm for God as the dogs have for the walk. I thought that is a bull's eye if ever there was one. If we can pull that off we will affect more people then passing out 1,000,000 tracts. We are called to let our light shine (Luke 8:16). Our enthusiasm for God pouring out of us is our bling. It's what catches the eye of the lost. You can change a life when others see something in you they want.

Dogs are like kids. They will use as much leash as you give them and strain for more. You only get them to heel well with constant training. According to the Dog Whisperer, "It is exercise, discipline and then affection." No dog enjoys the first two steps as much as the last step. No kid enjoys the discipline part of growing up. As the stepparent, I live on a slippery slope of acceptance. I want desperately to be loved "like a real parent," much like Pinocchio longed to be a real boy, but I need to maintain the role of parent and authority figure. My mother-in-law used to say we're their parents not their friends, which goes hand in hand with my mother telling me she didn't like us very much as teenagers before we became her best friends as adults.

Melisa said God was cramming it in because He didn't know when we'd be walking again. It's sad, but true. Our faithfulness to walk has fallen upon hard times. Our God is, as Melisa puts it, sitting on the front steps waiting for us to come out with the ladies, and more often than not the sun sets on him setting on the steps. I walk past Him on my way to my car to drive to work. He is the hitchhiker I need to pick up. We have a sign in Hinton, the town between Lookeba and Interstate 40 that says, "Hitchhikers may be escaped inmates." That sign, along with "Donkeys and Llamas for predator protection," cracked me up my first time to Western Oklahoma. There is no sign in my front yard by my step that warns against picking up anyone. I'm going to do a better job of giving God a lift every day even if we take a walk with Him in the morning.

I made a small contribution to today's walk. I got a song stuck in my head, "Indescribable" by Chris Tomlin. It talks about how God hung the stars in the sky and knows them by name. He gave us the sun and the cool of the night. I got to thinking, it's all His anyway. He's the superstar in the kindergarten class that doesn't need to be taught or reminded to share. He shares everything with anybody every day. We are in essence playing with the house's money. Anyone who's had a good day at the casino knows what a good feeling that is. Try looking at life from that perspective. See what kind of difference a little perspective change makes. You just might be surprised.

July 2nd
More Prayer

We spent most of the walk, much like yesterday, in prayer. It was funny. We paid almost no attention to the dogs and they behaved like they didn't need attention paid to them. We focused on the same three points as yesterday, partnership, prayer, and participation; the three factors for multiplication.

I was asking God about work and if he had ideas about what I needed to do to see more blessing there. His response was in keeping with the theme of gentle correction. His answer was that I'd brought Him to work and then left Him in my briefcase. When my Bible and books are left in my briefcase, I am leaving God out. When I leave God out of the equation, I get only as far as I can take myself.

The usual response when we get home is to wind down and pop on the television. Usually we watch a series of preaching. Today we decided to read the Word aloud ourselves. Oddly enough we finished, made the coffee, fed the dogs and completed our morning checklist just in time to watch our favorite morning preacher. The great thing about TV preaching is the networks will repeat the same show a couple of times of times a day so if we miss it because we are spending a little extra time in our conversation with God, we can catch our programs a little later. The sad thing about TV preaching is there aren't enough pastors with enough money to pay for TV time.

I do want to give some props to the canines. They were outstanding the last couple of days, despite some lazy, slovenly owners who preferred the comfort of their own bed to getting up and giving them the exercise they need. We let them down and they were loyal as dogs to us. They have not acted up and have been very good on the walk the last couple of days.

As we crested the big hill at the end of our walk, suddenly Dutchess stopped and pointed front leg bent, nose down, tail (what's left of it) pointed. I noticed the behavior, but was oblivious to the reason. There was a rabbit about three and a half feet away. It made me think what else is right in front of us that we miss. We don't have the heightened senses that Dutchess has so we have to be intentional about our awareness. I have to deal with the genetic predisposition towards being oblivious to things. My dad drove home this point when he stripped naked wearing only the daily paper and my mom walked in and out of the room twice without noticing. She got it on the third trip.

I love my mom and am without question my mother's son. That's why the dogs needed to bolt after the rabbit before I figured out what was going on three feet away. Let's be intentional about staying aware of what's going on. Here's an idea. If we are alert, we will become cognizant of the needs of others. We may not be able to meet all of them, but we will be able to meet some of them. You are hard pressed to meet a need you're unaware of. We have limited vision. In my case, really limited vision (thanks dad), and limited hearing. So we need to maximize what senses we do have so we can have the greatest effect on the people around us.

October 3ʳᵈ
Walking With The Stars

After a very long hiatus from walking the dogs, it is with great joy that I (Melisa) find myself the author of this entry. You see the reasons we have not been walking have been too numerous to list, but the biggest one is Steven's new job. It is truly a great blessing and we are very thankful for it. However, with every rose there are a few thorns. The biggest thorn in this rose of a job is the schedule. Now working 7am to 4pm, he must make the long trek into the city much earlier. He now leaves every morning at 5:30am. Lots of his faithful readers have questioned us about the latest entry in the Walking with God journal. Our standard response has been, "Are you crazy? As much as you love the journal we are not getting up at 4:00am to walk the dogs." So guess what, we didn't and for several weeks or a couple of months we have been unfaithful, slothful dog owners. But take heart. The dogs have now taken up your cause and they have made themselves pretty unpleasant to live with in an attempt to get us back on track with our daily walks. You know if God is willing to use a donkey to speak to someone I'm sure using a couple of Airedales is no problem for Him either (Numbers 22:22-35).

This morning was much different than most of the walks before. It was a girl's walk. The ladies and I headed out on the usual route. Yep, it was dark and we were alone, and I spent the first few blocks lamenting the fact that I was walking alone. Thinking about all the stories I'd ever heard about safety and wondering how great a plan walking the ladies alone in the dark was. Sometimes your thoughts can take you places you never really wanted to go. I began to do what I do most times when I have to face fear. I began to quote all the Scriptures I could think of about the protection of God. You know, God has given his angels charge over us (Hebrews 13:5), He never leaves nor forsakes us, he who dwells in the secret place of the most high shall abide under the shadow of the Almighty (Psalm 91)…you get the idea.

Then just as I rounded the third corner, the one that leads me out of town, I looked up to see the Northern Star. Not being great in astronomy, I am guessing that was the star I was seeing. Anyway for that moment it was the only star I saw. Then as I tilted my head back a little more I caught a glimpse of the moon, big and bright and very close to the star. God's way of reminding me I was not alone. Being very bright like the Northern Star, I quickly noticed that the moon was much bigger than the star. God's way of pointing out that He is much bigger than me, not to mention the fact that He is much bigger than my problem of walking alone with two dogs in the dark. You see, a lot of times life is about our focus. We can choose to focus on the size of our problems or we can choose to focus on the size of our God. Great to know we serve a big God. His word says He holds the universe in the palm of His hand. Sort of makes our biggest problems seem pretty small.

After noticing the size of the moon in comparison to the size of the star, my focus changed and I began to see that there were in fact many stars in the sky. God frequently speaks to me in mental pictures. Just at that moment, I got the picture of walking with four angels. There were two angels in front of me and two behind me. Now when I think of angels, I rarely think of them as the small and cute cherubs displayed in every gift shop around. I think of angels more like, The Hulk, strong and brave and totally ripped. The kind of angels that frequently keep my car from hitting other cars because they are pushing it back in to my lane as I multitask my way down the highway. I have long ago learned that my angels really do

Walking With God

need to have great strength and quick thinking to keep me safe, mostly from myself.

Then the thought came, why walk with four angels when I am really walking with God? Which lead to the mental picture of a king and his ante rouge. I saw God and a huge crowd of angels who followed him everywhere He went. Then the whole idea of walking alone seemed really silly. This was followed by the thought of the Cingular (now AT&T) commercials of the cell phone customer who has his network following him everywhere he went. It is true. God is the singular Creator of the universe and He does go with us wherever we go. What a peace we can have knowing that we are never alone. So the concept of walking with God was as clear as it has ever been.

Walking with the stars was more than just about walking with our personal stars, the Airedales, Elizabeth Taylor, and Dutchess of York. It was about walking with the Creator of the stars and the pure joy it brings to know that even when we can't see them, they are there and even though with our natural senses we cannot always see God we know that He is there. So try today to spend a little extra time remembering God is with you, He loves you and you are so wonderful He chooses never to leave you.

BACKWARD

You have bought the book, read it from front to back. It's time I come clean. I'm not the perfect pet owner destined for super-stardom and my own show on animal planet. I haven't continued to get up at 5am every day and walk the dogs. Melisa does a much better job at that than I do. We did do a stint in Airedale rescue and Melisa has brought our daughter into the next generation of canine companionship, helping with Great Dane rescue here in Oklahoma.

    This book has been a tribute to the wonderful things dogs can bring into your life. It is also a testimony to a loving God who will go to great lengths to do anything and use anything to pour into our lives His great love. My desire is that you find your breed, find your bible, and see what God wants to say to you as you go Walking With ~~Dog~~ God.

About the Author

While Steven Zimmerman is a relatively newcomer to the dog-owning world, he has been writing for years. Walking With ~~Dog~~ God is his first completed project with action thrillers, the great American novel, and poetry collections in various stages of completion. He and his wife, Melisa, are founders of Bridge Builders Marriage Ministry. They are at work on their next book, "Have Your Cake and Eat It Too – A Recipe for a Successful Marriage," coming to a marriage conference or bookstore near you.

www.ingramcontent.com/pod-product-compliance
Lightning Source LLC
Chambersburg PA
CBHW022015290426
44109CB00015B/1181